The Olympics of
Life

Ray Markham

Other books by Ray Markham:
What Kind of Power Is This?
(on the miracles of Jesus) ISBN 1-873796-92-7
Pointed and Personal
(on the parables of Jesus) ISBN 1-903921-04-X
Greater Expectations
(on the Sermon on the Mount) ISBN 1-903921-01-5
All published by Autumn House and come with questions for group study

Published by
The Leprosy Mission International
80 Windmill Road, Brentford
Middlesex TW8 0QH, United Kingdom

Edited and distributed by TLM Trading Limited
(Address on page 80)

All Bible quotations are from the New International Version, by permission
of The International Bible Society, unless otherwise stated.

First published 2003 © Ray Markham
Ray Markham has asserted his right to be identified as the author of this work in
accordance with the Copyright, Designs and Patents Act 1988.

All rights and subsidiary rights have been granted to
The Leprosy Mission International (see page 80 for contact details).

Editorial and Design by Craft Plus Publishing Ltd.
53 Crown Street, Brentwood, Essex CM14 4BD

Printed and bound in Spain by Bookprint, S.L. - Barcelona
A catalogue record for this book is available from the British Library.
ISBN 0-902731-48-3

Resources: *The Complete Book of the Olympics* by David Wallechinsky,
published by Aurum Press *(but now out of print)*;
www.times-olympics.co.uk www.olympics.org.
Picture credits: pages 30-31; 56-57, all Corbis UK

CONTENTS

FOREWORD

There can rarely have been a more epic Olympic moment! Carl Lewis and Ben Johnson on the blocks for the 100m final in Seoul, Korea, 1988. Johnson exploded off the line and through the tape to win by two metres – gold medal, world record, top of the world. BUT down he came with a shuddering crash. He tested positive as we all know, a steroid, performance enhancing. Goodnight Charlie, goodbye Ben. Olympics rocked to the core. And I was there! I was also there when Flojo sprinted to double gold – an astonishing and glamorous winner. Track and Field gets sexy! And now she is dead! They run, at very high cost it would seem, for a crown that does not last. They, well some of them, risk disqualification, judgement, by contaminating their bodies with banned substances. But beware the moral high ground! You see we are all running THE RACE contaminated by our wilful selfishness and sin. We all face disqualification at the Judgement. So what counts? Like Eric Liddell, run to celebrate God! His gift to you of a body that works, His creation of a playground, this beautiful world, in which to play. Looking to Jesus, with a gold medal that lasts around His neck, allow God to remake His marred image in you.

I stood in a chapel in the Olympic village in Seoul while a British cyclist introduced a Puerto Rican super heavyweight boxer to Jesus. I stood in a dentist's queue in the village in Sydney when a Kenyan 5,000 metre runner's face came alive with smiles as she told me "Oh Andrew, I love Jesus." I sat and prayed with Jonathan Edwards before he won his longed for gold medal, and he told me, "I am taking my triple jump to Jesus like the little boy who brought his loaves and fishes. Maybe He can do something with my futile gift!"

You will love these stories, anecdotes, reminiscences – enjoy! But remember "When you run you feel His pleasure."

In Jesus' team

Andrew – Oxford 2003

Andrew Wingfield Digby was Director of Christians in Sport from 1980 to 2002. He has served as an Olympic Chaplain twice and is spiritual adviser to the England team. He is now Vicar of St Andrew's Church in North Oxford and Chairman of Christians in Sport.

PREFACE

The Olympic Games! What do those three words conjure up in your mind? For me, it's excitement, drama, tragedy, agony, passion, triumph, despair, phenomenal achievements – and, of course, medals! Since the modern Olympics began back in 1896, they have never failed to produce remarkable stories about both the athletes themselves, and what happened during the events they took part in.

From this wealth of fascinating accounts, I have chosen those which illustrate various aspects of the Christian faith. Each section contains one or more stories which relate to a particular Biblical theme and give rise to a specific thought. My aim in writing this book was to re-tell these stories in an interesting and lively way, using them to stimulate thought and reflection in a way that will impact our daily lives. This makes it a book not just for those who love sport, but for all those who enjoy reading true-life stories, and are looking for something that is both compelling and thought-provoking. I have also included two indexes: one summarises the main themes contained in the 'thoughts'; the other lists the Bible references used in the book.

The motto of the Olympic movement is *Citius, Altius, Fortius*: swifter, higher, stronger. My prayer is that each person who reads these stories and thoughts will be spurred on to higher heights, deeper depths and greater experiences in God, as we take part in our own personal Olympics of Life.

Ray Markham, June 2003

DEDICATION

To my sporting family, especially my two sons Keith and Philip.

THE OLYMPICS OF LIFE

Every four years I have this dream. In this dream, I stand on a podium in a vast stadium, and have an Olympic gold medal hung round my neck. This time I'll be in Athens, the home of the Olympics. However, since I have neither the natural ability, nor an overwhelming desire to spend twenty-four hours in every day training, and am no longer in the first flush of youth, a dream is what it will forever remain.

But, when you think about it, we are all involved in our own, personal Olympics: the Olympics of Life. And there are no qualifying standards demanded for entry; you are in them, whether you like it or not! Some events require us to show speed of thought or movement. Some demand strength of character, while others require stamina and endurance. Some events need expert handling, others require a particular skill, and often the demands made on us are of Olympian proportions.

Some Olympic athletes have taken drugs to help them to win through. Many people take drugs too. Some smoke too much. Others can't get by without a few drinks under their belt. The use of cannabis, cocaine, heroin and other drugs is on the increase. Some people simply run away from their problems, or always put them off till tomorrow; and tomorrow never comes.

Such drugs can make us believe that we are going to win through. But, eventually, they all wear off, and the events of life are still going on. And we find to our dismay that we are needed for another event while we're still involved in the present one! There are no rules laid down by a committee for the Olympics of Life.

Australian swimmer, Grant Hackett, experienced this kind of pressure at the 2000 Games in Sydney. Although he won the gold medal in the 1,500 metres freestyle, he was very disappointed with his performance in the 200 and 400 metres events, which he had swum in earlier. He blamed his failure to come up to expectations on being in too many events at the same Olympics. In his opinion, the same applied to another swimmer. In a radio interview he said, "We saw Susie O'Neill beaten in the 200 metres butterfly, and I think she was another case of somebody who had too many races and too many events. I wish I hadn't had the 200 freestyle and had a couple of days to rest after the 400 metres free."

How can we possibly cope with the pressure of every day life? We need help and strength that is lasting, and not just effective for one 'event' only; God alone can supply this. The Bible tells us that God will give us all the strength and peace of mind that we are lacking [Psalm 29:11].

Unlike me, Eric Liddell did achieve his Olympic dream *(see photo on page 30)*. At the 1924 Games held in Paris, the Scotsman won the gold medal in the 400 metres in a new Olympic record time, as well as the bronze medal in the 200 metres. He was one of the athletes featured in the film *Chariots of Fire*. In 1925, he returned to China to work alongside his father on the mission field. He was in China during the Second World War, and was captured by the Japanese. He died of a brain tumour in the Weifang internment camp on 21st February 1945, and his body was laid in an unmarked grave. He lived and died serving God.

In 1990, the grave was located by Charles Walker, a civil engineer based in Hong Kong. On 9th June the following year, a monument made out of Scottish granite was erected in Weifang in Eric Liddell's honour. On it were inscribed these words from the book of Isaiah: 'They shall mount up with wings as eagles; they shall run, and not be weary' [40:31 AV].

Eric Liddell knew, and so can we, that by God's strength and grace we can compete with confidence in the Olympics of Life.

Prayer

Father God, I need your strength to help me through each day.

Sometimes I feel as if I'm never going to make it.

Sometimes I feel that it's just not worth the effort any more.

Father, when I feel like this, let me know your presence with me in a very real way, strengthening me and enabling me to face whatever lies ahead.

Amen.

A FRIENDLY PIECE OF WOOD

Participating in sport seems to bring out the superstitious side in many of us. There's the player who always puts his kit on in the same order, even down to which shoe or boot is tied first. Some teams always run out onto the field in the same order, with the same players carrying the balls. Some players refuse to wear the 'unlucky' number 13 shirt, while others crave the 'lucky' number 7. There is no end to the different rituals which are carried out wherever the drama that is sport is played out.

According to the Oxford English Dictionary, superstitious activity is 'irrational' and 'unreasoning'. So, why do many of those taking part in sport behave in this way? For me the answer is simple enough: to get the edge over their opponents, and thereby to come out the winner. They're really saying: "If there's something out there, I want it on *my* side!" And that 'something' is often personified and given a name: Lady Luck.

Athletes taking part in the Olympic Games are no exception to this. Kate Howey of Great Britain, a competitor in the 70kg class of the judo event at the 2000 Games, was horrified to find that she had left her lucky fighting belt behind. Her team-mate, Vicki Dunn, raced back to the Olympic village and began a frantic search for the belt. Eventually she found it and got back to the venue just in time. With her lucky belt firmly in place, Howey went on to win the silver medal.

At the 1920 Games held in Antwerp, the winner of the gold medal in the 100 metres was the American sprinter, Charley Paddock. He was a great favourite with the crowds, and especially with the photographers, due to his 'flying finish', in which he would fling his arms high and wide and leap at the tape from about 4 yards out. In the course of preparing himself for a race, Paddock would do something very unusual. As he approached the starting line, he would knock on what he described as 'a friendly piece of wood'. Then, when settling to his mark, he would place his hands in front of him as far as he could reach, and then draw them slowly back into the correct position just before the starter called "Get set".

He went through this ritual every time he ran, but at the start of the Olympic final, something else occurred which shows the lengths to which competitors will go to keep the edge over their opponents. Just before they were called for the race, the American coach, Lawson Robertson, approached the four American athletes who were in the final and said, "What you fellows need to warm up is a glass of sherry and a raw egg." Murchison, Paddock and Sholz were horrified at this suggestion, but Morris Kirksey drank his straight down. The other three, fearing that this might give Kirksey a psychological advantage, promptly did the same!

On his visit to Athens, the apostle Paul encountered all manner of religions, beliefs and superstitions. But what particularly took his eye was an altar with the inscription: TO AN UNKNOWN GOD. The people of Athens were so anxious to keep on the right side of anything that might be 'out there' that they had covered any omissions they may have inadvertently made by constructing this altar. They wanted to make sure that any supernatural force that existed was on their side, and was not angry with them.

Paul wrote, 'Now what you worship as something unknown I am going to proclaim to you' [Acts 17:23]. And he did, telling them about the one true God who created the world and everything in it; who is so awesome that no human temple could contain him; and who gave breath and life to all of creation. And God did all this, said Paul, for a particular reason: 'so that men would seek him and perhaps reach out for him and find him, though he is not far from each one of us. "For in him we live and move and have our being"'[17:27-28].

How wonderful to know that God's desire is that we *find* him, not *fear* him; that he wants to be *known* personally by us, not to be an *unknown* power somewhere 'out there', that can be persuaded to be on our side if we perform certain rituals. On the contrary: his love has done all that needs to be done; all we have to do is to love him in return.

Prayer

Thank you, Father, that you want us not only to find you, but also to know you more day by day.

Thank you for being a personal, loving, caring God, who is not only on my side, but also at my side forever. Help me to place my trust in you and not in some irrational superstition.

Amen.

A SUBTLE BLEND

They say that the media never let the truth get in the way of a good story! The film *Chariots of Fire* tells the story of a group of athletes as they prepare for and take part in the 1924 Games held in Paris. It focuses particularly on three of them: Harold Abrahams, Lord David Burghley and Eric Liddell. Unfortunately, this otherwise excellent film contains certain factual inaccuracies.

For example, what drove Harold Abrahams was not so much that he felt an outsider because he was a Jew, but the fact that he wanted to outdo his two older brothers, who had both taken part in previous Olympics. Nor did Abrahams run round the great courtyard of Trinity College at Cambridge in the time it took the clock to strike 12 o'clock. This feat was, in fact, accomplished in 1927 by Lord Burghley. His Lordship was 76 years old when the film came out, and was understandably upset that his feat had been attributed to Abrahams, even to the point of refusing to see the film. Nor did Lord Burghley put a glass of champagne on each hurdle and practise leaping over them without spilling a drop. In fact, he put a matchbox on each one and practised knocking them off with his lead foot without touching the hurdle.

And what of Eric Liddell? In fact, he knew six months in advance, and not at the last minute, that the final of the 100 metres would take place on a Sunday, so he had plenty of time to adjust his training for the 200 and 400 metres instead *(see photo on page 30)*. Not to mention the fact that Lord Burghley was never even entered for the 400 metres, so he didn't withdraw and give his place to Liddell at all.

And as for the encouraging note with the words 'Those who honour me I will honour' [1 Samuel 2:30], supposedly handed to Liddell by Jackson Scholz just before he ran in the final of the 400 – that, I'm afraid, was also a complete fantasy!

The inclusion of this inaccuracy in the film actually caused considerable embarrassment for Jackson, who was not a religious man. When the film was released, he was 84 years old, and was overwhelmed by the amount of mail he received from people asking for spiritual inspiration!

I wonder how many people actually had the temerity to question the film's factual accuracy? I know I didn't! I just accepted it as the truth, because people who I assumed knew what they were talking about, and could be trusted, had told me. How wrong I was! In fact, what I had been served up was a subtle blend of truth and error. I'm sure the scriptwriters did not set out deliberately to deceive but to give us a good and compelling story, and succeeded admirably. Nevertheless, error had been accepted as truth.

Jesus knew that, down the years, the church would be infiltrated by many false prophets, who would bring teachings that were a subtle blend of truth and error, leading many Christians astray. Unlike the film scriptwriters though, the intention of these teachers was indeed deception. He warned his disciples to be constantly on the lookout for such people [Matthew 7:15, see also Matthew 24:11,24].

False prophets were active in the early church and are still active today. Paul wrote about them [2 Corinthians 11:13]; but it is Peter who really goes to town on this subject. He warns about 'destructive heresies', and that 'these teachers will exploit you with stories they have made up' [2 Peter 2:1-3].

In spite of these warnings not to be deceived, it is evident that many Christians still are, often with drastic consequences. Just count the numerous sects and cults that have sprung up in recent years. We need to be on our guard, and to test everything we hear and read against the truth of what the Bible teaches, irrespective of where the words are coming from.

Prayer

Father God, thank you for all the warnings contained in your Word about false teaching.

Forgive me for the times I have not tested what I have read or been told against the truth of your Word.

Thank you, Father, that your Word is true and unchanging, and that I can put my trust in it completely.

I pray for any who may be suffering as a result of accepting such false teaching. May they be speedily restored to you.

Amen.

SERIOUS PREPARATION

Like all Olympic athletes, Harold Abrahams took his training very seriously indeed. To get the length of his strides absolutely right, he would meticulously place pieces of paper on the track to indicate where each stride should end. Then he would practise running in such a way that the spikes of his running shoes would pick up all the pieces as he ran. (I'm not sure how he got on when it was windy!) Then, before an actual race, he would take a piece of string, which had been cut to the length of his first stride, and measure out that precise distance from the start, making a mark on the track where his foot should land.

For sheer dedication to training in preparation for his event, American athlete Dan Gable takes some beating. He trained seven hours a day, every day, for three years leading up to the 1972 Games held in Munich, where he won the gold medal in the lightweight division of the freestyle wrestling. As a teenager, his training included mowing the lawn, running, while wearing a rubber suit along with weights on his arms and legs!

British athlete Don Thompson had been taught a sharp lesson about the importance of meticulous preparation when he took part in the 50 kilometre walk at the Melbourne Games in 1956. He was in fifth place with 5,000 metres to go when he collapsed and was unable to finish. Aware that the 1960 Games would be held in Rome, where the conditions were likely to be hot and humid, he decided on an ingenious way of preparing for these conditions. He sealed the bathroom door and windows, and created an environment of 38°C (100°F) by means of heaters, boiling kettles and hot water in the bath. He then proceeded to do his training in these conditions.

When the day of the race came, it was indeed hot and humid, but Thompson was ready. He stormed to victory, winning the gold medal in a time of 4 hours 25 minutes and 30 seconds, a new Olympic record. All those years of serious preparation had borne fruit.

We also need to be thoroughly prepared for those hot and humid times we often find ourselves in, many of which bring storms into our lives. The tree with deep roots has the best chance of surviving even the fiercest tempest. In the same way, there is no substitute for being deeply rooted and grounded in God's Word, so that when those times of testing come, we can stand firm. In my experience, this can only be achieved through spending time regularly meditating on what the Bible says, otherwise I am in danger of becoming like the rocky ground, where the seed fell and started to grow, but then shrivelled in the heat of the sun [Matthew 13:5-6; 20-21].

Because of their thorough preparation, Abrahams, Gable and Thompson were able to grasp the opportunities they were given. God gives us opportunities to witness for him; another reason for spending time in the training ground of God's Word. As Peter wrote: 'Always be prepared to give an answer to everyone who asks you to give the reason for the hope that you have' [1 Peter 3:15].

Even though there must be times when all athletes find it difficult to maintain a high level of enthusiasm for their training, they are so convinced of their need to be thoroughly prepared that they are willing to make the effort required. According to surveys carried out by the organisation Scripture Union, fewer than 20% of Christians bother to read their Bible regularly. Imagine the difference it would make to our lives and witness if only we all had the same serious commitment to knowing God's Word as these athletes had to their preparation and training.

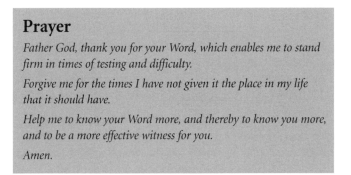

Prayer

Father God, thank you for your Word, which enables me to stand firm in times of testing and difficulty.

Forgive me for the times I have not given it the place in my life that it should have.

Help me to know your Word more, and thereby to know you more, and to be a more effective witness for you.

Amen.

FIXED FOCUS

The climax to Harold Abrahams' meticulous preparation and training for the 100 metres came at 7.05 pm on the 7th of July 1924, as he took his place at the start of the final. Lining up with him were the Americans Charley Paddock, gold medal winner in this event at the 1920 Games, Jackson Scholz, Chester Bowman and Loren Murchison, along with Arthur Porritt of New Zealand. Although Abrahams had recorded the fastest times in the previous rounds, the Americans were still the favourites. Realising that he had a very good chance of winning the gold medal, Abrahams began to feel the pressure as the time for the final drew near. Later, he recalled that he "felt like a condemned man feels just before going to the scaffold."

Having used his piece of string to measure where his first stride should land, and marked the spot, Abrahams took his place at the start line. As he did so, he called to mind the final words of advice given to him by his down-to-earth coach, Sam Mussabini: "Only think of two things – the report of the pistol and the tape. When you hear the one, just run like hell till you break the other." Abrahams won the race by a margin of two feet in a time of 10.6 seconds, which equalled the Olympic record. Scholz took the silver and Porritt the bronze.

At the 1928 Games held in Amsterdam, the final of the 400 metres was expected to be a close contest between James Ball of Canada and Joachim Buchner of Germany. However, as they came into the final straight, the American runner Ray Barbuti was in the lead. Ball unleashed a great finishing kick and, as they approached the tape, he was within a foot of Barbuti. It was at this point that Ball made a costly mistake; he took his eyes off the tape and looked sideways to his left to see where Barbuti was. At that precise moment, Barbuti lunged for the tape and fell to the ground, scraping his arm, leg and side – but he had won the gold medal, leaving Ball in second place. Later, Barbuti told reporters: "I never noticed the other runners after the start. I heard them, but all I kept thinking was 'run, kid, run'. I don't remember anything of the last 100 metres except a mad desire to get to that tape."

The apostle Paul exhorts us to have that same 'mad desire to get to the tape' as Barbuti had. 'Do you not know that in a race all the runners run, but only one gets the prize? Run in such a way as to get the prize. Everyone who competes in the games goes into strict training. They do it to get a crown that will not last; but we do it to get a crown that will last for ever' [1 Corinthians 9:24-25].

Barbuti and Abrahams had a focus, and they fixed their eyes intently on it. Our focus is not a tape; the race we are in is not for earthly reward. The focus of our race is the Lord Jesus himself. 'Let us fix our eyes on Jesus', says the writer to the Hebrews [12:2]. And it is our Lord's desire to bestow the heavenly reward of 'a crown that will last for ever' on each one of us, not just on one of us. But to gain that 'crown', Jesus must remain the focus of our lives. It is so easy to make the same costly mistake as James Ball: allowing ourselves to be distracted, and getting caught up with what's going on around us, thus taking our eyes off Jesus – often with dire consequences.

It is so important that we check where our eyes are looking, to make sure that they are focused on Jesus only. The direction of our eyes determines the direction we take. The focus of our lives can be clearly seen by what we 'run after' [Matthew 6:31-33]. In that passage, Jesus challenges us to think about whether we are running after the things of the world, or the things of the Kingdom.

In everything he said and did, Paul's focus was on Jesus. So he could say of himself, 'Therefore I do not run like a man running aimlessly…' [1 Corinthians 9:26]. I wonder if the same can be said of us? Jesus himself had a focus. Luke tells us: 'As the time approached for him to be taken up to heaven, Jesus resolutely set out for Jerusalem' [Luke 9:51], knowing that he was going to certain death on a cross, and he let nothing distract him or deflect him from that focus. And because Jesus went to the cross, wearing the crown of thorns, we can wear the crown of life.

Prayer

Lord Jesus, thank you that your focus on the cross means that I can have eternal life.

May you and you alone be the focus of my life always, in all I say and do.

Forgive me for the times I run after the things of the world, rather than seeking first your Kingdom.

Help me to live my life with the aim and purpose of serving you and you alone.

Amen.

TIMING

Although Valery Borzov from the Ukraine was the overwhelming favourite for the gold medal in the 100 metres at the 1972 Games in Munich, both Eddie Hart from California and Rey Robinson from Florida had recorded a time of 9.9 seconds at the US Olympic trials. Borzov, Hart and Robinson each won their respective heats in the first round during the morning of the 31st August, and another American sprinter, Robert Taylor, also qualified. The next round was due to begin at 4.15 that same afternoon.

Lee Evans, who had won the 400 metres gold medal at the 1968 Games in Mexico City, began to worry when he couldn't see his three compatriots anywhere in the stadium as the time for the quarter finals drew near. He tried the warm-up track, but with no success. The Olympic Village was about three-quarters of a mile away, so Evans ran there as fast as he could, but still he couldn't find them. In fact, they and their coach, Stan Wright, had just left to catch the bus for the stadium, thinking that the quarter finals started at 7 pm. Unfortunately, Wright was working from an outdated preliminary schedule produced 18 months before the Games.

While waiting for the bus, they sauntered into the doorway of the ABC-TV headquarters and began to watch the television monitor. They saw runners lining up for the start of the 100 metres and thought they were seeing a re-run of the first round. When they found out that they were actually watching a live transmission, they were horrified. Robinson realised that the heat he was watching was the one he was supposed to be running in! ABC employee Bill Norris rushed them to the stadium in his car, but it was too late for Robinson and also for Hart, who was due to run in the second heat. They were both eliminated. Taylor was just in time for his heat and finished second behind Borzov. In the final held the next day, Taylor finished behind Borzov again, but he won the silver medal.

Ralph Boston of the United States was the strong favourite to take the gold medal in the long jump at the 1964 Games in Tokyo. He was the defending Olympic champion and the world record holder. Nobody really gave Lynn Davies of Great Britain a chance. But the weather was to play a crucial role. It was cold, wet and windy, something that Davies was used to coming from Wales, whereas Boston and the other finalists were not. After four rounds, Davies was lying in third place. Later, he recalled his thoughts as he prepared for his fifth round jump. "I remember thinking, this is it. I glanced up at the flag at the top of the stadium. Boston told me about this in New York, four months previously. 'If the flag drops,' he had said, 'it's a good indication that the wind is about to fade inside the stadium.' And as I looked up at it, it dropped dead." Davies seized the moment, raced down the runway and jumped further than he'd ever done before. 'Lynn the Leap', as the British newspapers dubbed him, had got his timing just right and had won the gold medal.

Unlike Davies, the American coach got his timing wrong, with disastrous consequences for the athletes under his care. But God's timing is always perfect; he always gets it right! How often do we look back on our lives and have to admit that God's timing of events was perfect, although we weren't convinced at the time! And all because we are under his care.

Paul tells us more about God's perfect timing. 'But when the time had fully come, God sent his Son, born of a woman…' [Galatians 4:4]. Jesus was born at precisely the right time in history for the events of his life to unfold, and for the Gospel, which he came to bring, to be spread throughout the known world. And we can be confident that the timing of Jesus' second coming, this time in power and glory, will be just as perfect as that of his first coming.

Down the ages, people have sought to predict the timing of his return, but Jesus told us quite clearly that 'No-one knows about that day or hour, not even the angels in heaven, nor the Son, but only the Father' [Mark 13:32]. He followed these words with a short parable, urging us to go about our God-given tasks, but at the same time to be watching for his return. This means living our lives in the expectation that Jesus will return today, which will dictate our priorities, and making sure we are ready for his coming by both serving him faithfully, and by burning brightly for him in this dark world.

Prayer

Thank you, Father, that your timing is always perfect.

Thank you for the times in my life when I have experienced your loving care in this way.

Help me to serve you faithfully and to shine brightly until the time comes for your return.

Amen.

MASKING THE TRUTH

One of the most famous athletes in the history of the Olympic Games is undoubtedly the American, James 'Jesse' Owens *(see photo on page 30)*. Nicknamed 'The Ebony Antelope', he became the first athlete to win four gold medals at the same Games. At the 1936 Berlin Olympics he won the 100 metres, the 200 metres and the long jump; then he ran the first leg of the 4 x 100 metres relay, helping the team to win gold in a world record time of 39.8 seconds. When asked about the secret of his success, he told a reporter, "I let my feet spend as little time on the ground as possible. From the air, fast down, and from the ground, fast up. My foot is only a fraction of the time on the track". His feat remained unequalled until the 1984 Games in Los Angeles, when another American, Carl Lewis, won gold in the same four events.

Adolf Hitler had set out to use the Berlin Games as a platform on which to demonstrate the superiority of the Aryan race. Indeed, Nazi propaganda prior to the Games had portrayed Negroes as inferior. The achievements of Owens certainly showed up this Nazi philosophy for what it was. Hitler was no doubt annoyed by Owens' successes, but the story that he snubbed him by refusing to meet him is apparently not true. However, Owens was snubbed by a world leader – his own President! Although welcomed home as a hero in America, receiving tickertape parades in New York City and in his home town of Cleveland, unbelievably President Franklin Delano Roosevelt never invited him to the White House, nor even sent him a letter of congratulations. He was also passed over for the Sullivan award, which was given to the best American amateur athlete of the year.

However, in the years that followed, Owens was presented as the archetypal clean-living, honest-to-goodness hero that American society craved. But the truth was rather different. For example, Owens had various mistresses, was convicted for the non-payment of taxes, and smoked a pack of cigarettes a day for 35 years, eventually dying of lung cancer in 1980. Also, Owens invented the sort of details about his life that the public wanted to hear. In the end, he even included the Hitler snub myth in his speeches because the American public believed it was true, although he had always insisted that it had never happened.

In the theatre of Ancient Greece, the actors would come on stage holding a painted mask of the face of the character they were portraying in front of their own. In this way, the person could pretend to be someone they were not. The Greek word for such a masked actor is 'hypocrite'.

Jesus' constant complaint against the Pharisees was that they said one thing and did another. They put on an act in public, which was not borne out in private [Matthew 23:25-28]. That's why Jesus often used the term 'hypocrites' to describe them. It is very challenging to consider how we measure up to this test. Are our words and actions in harmony, or is there a discord? Does the image we present on the public stage square with the way we conduct ourselves in our private lives? Is the verdict of the God who sees all and knows all the same for us as it was for the Pharisees?

In a scenario taken straight out of his father's carpentry workshop in Nazareth, Jesus identified other areas of hypocrisy that we need to address: pretending to have no faults when we have as many as anyone else; pretending to be right in the sight of God when we're not. Jesus doesn't mince his words. 'You hypocrite', he says to us, 'first take the plank out of your own eye, and then you will see clearly to remove the speck from your brother's eye' [Matthew 7:5]. In other words, don't judge others, but do judge yourself; and then take the appropriate action to deal with the faults and shortcomings identified through this self-examination. Significantly, Jesus expects us to do this 'first', before trying to help our 'brother' to deal with his faults.

A common taunt directed at the church today is that it is full of hypocrites. May God help us to get our act together, and to live lives of integrity that are pleasing to him. Only then can we be effective ambassadors for Christ in the world in which we live [2 Corinthians 5:20].

Prayer

Father God, forgive me for the times when my actions have not been in harmony with my words; for the times when the image I have presented in public has not been a true reflection of my private life; for the times when I have judged others rather than judging myself; for the times when I have pretended to be right in your sight when I haven't been.

Father, please strengthen me, help me, and give me your wisdom as I seek to deal with the areas and attitudes in my life that are not pleasing to you, that I might live a life of integrity before you.

Amen.

PAYING THE PRICE

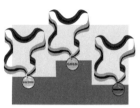

The 1976, 1980 and 1984 Olympic Games, held in Montreal, Moscow and Los Angeles respectively, each suffered due to boycotts by particular groups of nations. In 1976, 22 black African nations boycotted the Olympics because a New Zealand rugby team had toured South Africa, a country which was excluded from all international sport due to their policy of apartheid.

In 1980, the Games were subject to a boycott led by the President of the USA, Jimmy Carter. This was part of a range of measures put together to protest at the Soviet invasion of Afghanistan, which had occurred in December 1979. Some governments, such as the United Kingdom and Australia, supported the boycott, but allowed their athletes to make the final decision for themselves. Sebastian Coe and Steve Ovett were among those from the UK who resisted the pressure applied by Prime Minister Margaret Thatcher, and decided to go to Moscow. Athletes from the USA were allowed no such choice, with President Carter threatening to revoke the passport of anyone who decided to go to Moscow. In the end, 65 nations boycotted the 1980 Games, which meant that only 80 countries took part, the lowest number since 1956. The sports that suffered the most from the boycott were yachting, field hockey, men's swimming and the equestrian events.

When it was announced that the next Olympics were to take place in the USA, it came as a surprise to no-one that the Soviet Union decided to take revenge and lead a boycott of the 1984 Los Angeles Games. Although only 14 nations refused their invitations to attend, the sports of weightlifting, freestyle wrestling, gymnastics, team handball, modern pentathlon and the women's track and field events were badly hit.

It must have been heartbreaking for all the individual athletes who suffered because they belonged to a boycotting nation, especially for those with a realistic chance of winning a medal. How must they have felt, having trained so hard and with such dedication over many years, to have their life's ambition suddenly snatched away, simply because of their nationality? Unless we've actually been in that position, we can't begin to imagine.

We can only sympathise with athletes such as John Akii-Bua, Filbert Bayi, Renaldo Nehemiah, Greg Foster, Edwin Moses, Tracey Wickham, Sergei Bubka and Jarmila Kratochvilova, not to mention the US basketball team and the ladies' gymnastics team from the Soviet Union. They and many others had no option but to sit there and watch on TV as the medals they could have won were being awarded to someone else. That was the price they had to pay for belonging to a particular nation.

Peter tells us that we are 'a holy nation, a people belonging to God' [1 Peter 2:9]. Jesus made it very clear that belonging to this holy nation is a costly business; there is a price to be paid. He said, 'If anyone would come after me, he must deny himself and take up his cross and follow me' [Mark 8:34]. The athletes were expected to obey the leaders of their nations. As members of God's holy nation, we are expected to be obedient to King Jesus. This means that we are to give up any notion of doing things our way any more. We are to submit ourselves to the Lordship of Christ, obeying his commands, identifying ourselves with him, and becoming his servants. Paul goes so far as to use the picture of slavery to describe what is required of us [Romans 6:15-23].

Doing what God wants us to do can be costly and demand sacrifices on our part. We might be called upon to turn the other cheek, or to go the extra mile [Matthew 5:38-42]. Identifying ourselves with Jesus often comes at the cost of opposition, and in some parts of the world, persecution. That's why Jesus advised us to weigh up the implications of becoming his disciple carefully before making the decision [Luke 14:25-33]. And yet, what greater joy is there than serving the King of Kings, and being a subject of his holy nation?

Prayer

Thank you, Father, that I belong to your holy nation, and for the joy that there is to be found in serving you.

Jesus, I submit to your Lordship; have your way in my life I pray.

Help me to be obedient to your commands, especially those I find difficult and costly.

I lift before you all those who are facing persecution today because of their allegiance to you. Comfort and strengthen them I pray.

Amen.

FOUND OUT

It was at the 1988 Games held in Seoul that the whole issue of drugs hit the headlines, mainly due to the fact that one of the athletes who was caught was the winner of the gold medal in the 100 metres – Ben Johnson. But the use of performance-enhancing drugs had been going on almost since the Games began. For example, Thomas Hicks, the winner of the 1904 marathon, was given multiple doses of strychnine and brandy during the actual race! In 1968, Hans-Gunnar Liljenwall, a member of the Swedish modern pentathlon team, was disqualified for using alcohol. And it is now an established fact that the coaches of the East German teams carried out a widespread drug enhancement programme between 1968 and 1989.

In fact, Ben Johnson was the 43rd Olympic athlete to be disqualified for taking drugs since testing began in 1968, but he was the first 'big fish' to be caught, causing an enormous 'splash', which made a huge impact in the world of sport. Suspicions about Johnson had been raised back in 1987, when he broke the world record by a full tenth of a second at the world championships, clocking 9.83 seconds and beating his great rival Carl Lewis. Indeed, on the track circuit Johnson was known as 'Benoid', due to his highly sculptured muscles and yellow-tinged eyes – both indications that he was using steroids. As the runners took their marks for the 1988 Olympic final, it is said that Johnson's muscles were so highly developed that 'they seemed to be separate beings on the verge of exploding out of his skin'. Not surprisingly, he won by a huge margin in the breathtaking time of 9.79 seconds, a new world record.

Lewis, who had always been convinced that Johnson was on steroids, was angry that his rival seemed to have got away with it yet again. He wanted to protest, but thought better of it. When Johnson's urine sample proved positive, the disgraced athlete had to face the world's press and confess his wrong-doing. He was stripped of the gold medal, which was awarded to Lewis, who thus became the first man to win the 100 metres twice, having previously taken gold in 1984.

There is a verse in the book of Numbers which says, 'you may be sure that your sin will find you out' [32:23]. Ben Johnson thought he had got away with it as he took the plaudits of the crowd on that day in Seoul. He had got away with it before and I'm sure he was confident that he would never be caught. But the very next day, his wrong-doing was exposed; he had been found out.

Western society today seems to have lost all sense of sin. Wrong-doing isn't something to be ashamed of any more; it's something to 'get away with'. But ultimately, we will all be found out. Although our sins may not be exposed publicly, as in the case of Ben Johnson, they lie exposed before an all-seeing God, to whom we are all accountable.

It can be easy to fool other people, as Johnson did for so long, but we can never fool God. How important it is, then, that we confess our sins and don't try to cover them up in the hope that we'll get away with them, as Ben Johnson tried to. And isn't it wonderful to know that, whatever sins we may have committed, if we repent and confess them before God, he 'will forgive us our sins and purify us from all unrighteousness' [1 John 1:9].

There may be times when, like Carl Lewis, we feel angry that the wicked seem to prosper and evil goes unpunished. Many of the Psalmists felt exactly the same, but came to the realisation that this was only a temporary situation; one day each person would be judged by God. As Paul reminds us: 'For we must all appear before the judgement seat of Christ, that each one may receive what is due to him for the things done while in the body, whether good or bad' [2 Corinthians 5:10].

I praise God for the day when I 'found out' about his grace, mercy and love for me. Now I no longer fear his judgement, but rather rejoice in his forgiveness.

Prayer

Father God, I lift my country up to you, and ask that you would restore among us a sense of sin and the need to get right with you.

In your name I come against the wickedness and evil that is present in society, and ask that you will move in this nation through the power of your Spirit.

Father, forgive me for the times I have not confessed my sin before you.

Thank you for your unfailing grace, mercy, love and forgiveness.

Amen.

BODY MATTERS

It was at the 1976 Games in Montreal that the women's swimming team from East Germany first hit the headlines. Having failed to win a single gold medal at the 1972 Games, there they were winning 11 out of the 13 events in the pool. They repeated this feat at the 1980 Games in Moscow. Having been part of the Soviet boycott in 1984, they returned for the 1988 Games in Seoul, where Kristin Otto won six gold medals. Their dramatic success in Montreal had made many people think that they must be taking prohibited performance-enhancing drugs, a suspicion which was ultimately proved to be true in the 1990s.

It emerged that many of these girls had been given steroids without them knowing it before they reached puberty. They were under strict instructions not to tell their parents about the 'little blue pills' they were swallowing. A high percentage of them suffered severe health problems in later life. In fact, in the year 2000, Lothar Kipke, the chief doctor of the East German Swimming Federation from 1975 to 1985, was convicted of causing bodily harm to 58 swimmers.

What happened to these girls is perhaps the clearest example of the severe consequences that taking performance-enhancing drugs can have for the athlete. Indeed, there are times when the consequences have been fatal. For example, at the 1960 Games held in Rome, a Danish cyclist named Knut Jensen died during the road race due to ingesting amphetamines and nicotinyl tartrate.

Other athletes have suffered in later life because of the training regime their bodies have endured. Perhaps the best example of this is Volodymyr Kuts of the Soviet Union, who was the gold medallist at the 1956 Melbourne Games in both the 5,000 and 10,000 metres. He had been put through an experimental training programme by the Soviet coaches over a period of time, which eventually took its toll. In 1960, Kuts suffered his first heart attack and died as a result of his fourth heart attack in 1975.

Every athlete knows that what they do with their body matters, as do their families; just ask the surviving East German girl swimmers, and the relatives of Knut Jensen and Volodymyr Kuts. The apostle Paul tells all Christians that what we do with our body matters too. In his first letter to the Corinthians he wrote, 'Do you not know that your body is a temple of the Holy Spirit, who is in you, whom you have received from God? You are not your own; you were bought at a price. Therefore honour God with your body' [1 Corinthians 6:19-20].

Paul is saying that since the Spirit of God, who is holy, now lives within us, we need to think seriously whether what we do with our body renders it a fit place for him to dwell in. Now that we actually belong to God and not to ourselves any more, everything we do with and to our body is to honour God, since it is now his dwelling place.

Although Paul was referring specifically to sexual immorality, which is expressly forbidden throughout the Bible, it seems to me that the whole tenor of Scripture requires us to be careful in all matters concerning our body. Since there are no definitive teachings about many of these body matters, Christians differ in their understanding of what is acceptable to God and what isn't. Each one of us needs to pray these matters through before the Lord, with a willingness of heart to make any necessary changes to our lifestyle.

Personally, I find it helpful to ask myself these two questions when considering body matters: "Does what I am doing please and honour a holy God?" and "Would Jesus have done this with his body?" For we know that if we honour God in all things (and that includes body matters), then he will honour us [1 Samuel 2:30].

Prayer

Lord Jesus, thank you for the price you paid to redeem me.

Now that I belong to you, please give me wisdom in the decisions I make concerning my body, that it may always be a temple in which you are pleased to dwell.

Lord, may I honour you in this and in all things.

Amen.

CLENCHED FISTS

When Australian runner Peter Norman, a Salvation Army officer and teacher of physical education, travelled to Mexico City to take part in the 1968 Games, he can hardly have imagined that he would be caught up in a sensational incident which would have repercussions around the world.

In the heats of the 200 metres, Norman clocked an Olympic record time of 20.2 seconds and found himself in the final alongside the two favourites, Tommie Smith and John Carlos of the USA. Carlos was the current holder of the world record in this event. Both Smith and Carlos went to the San Hose State College in California and they were both members of the Olympic Project for Human Rights, an organisation of black athletes formed to protest about the treatment of black people in the USA.

Smith, who had pulled a muscle in his groin in the semi-final, found himself a yard and a half down on Carlos as they came off the bend and into the straight. It was then that Smith turned on what became known as his 'Tommie-jets' and, in an unforgettable display of power sprinting, he surged past Carlos with 60 metres still to go and took the gold in a new world record time of 19.83 seconds. Carlos was distracted by Smith passing him, allowing Norman to lunge at the tape and claim the silver ahead of him, leaving Carlos with the bronze.

But the sensation caused by the manner of Smith's win was nothing to that caused by the actions of Smith and Carlos at the medal ceremony. They both wore civil rights buttons and stood barefoot on the podium. Around his neck Smith wore a black scarf and Carlos wore a string of beads, both in memory of all those blacks who had been lynched. When the American national anthem was played, they both bowed their heads and raised a black-gloved fist in the Black Power salute.

The clenched fists stood for black strength and unity, and the bare feet were a symbol of the poverty of black people in the United States. Their bowed heads showed that they believed the words about freedom expressed in the anthem were only valid for white Americans, not black.

Peter Norman must have found himself in a very difficult and awkward position. He decided to co-operate with Smith and Carlos to the extent that he agreed to wear a civil rights button at the medal ceremony. When asked why he had gone along with the other two, Norman replied that he supported human rights and was against the 'white Australia' policy of his own government *(see photo on page 30)*.

It was okay for Smith to raise two clenched fists in victory as he crossed the finishing line, but as soon as he raised one clenched fist in protest, he was thrown out of the Games, along with Carlos. The international response to their protest was, on the whole, sympathetic but back home in the USA it was viewed rather differently in many quarters. For a while, Smith and Carlos found it difficult to get a job and both their marriages broke up.

Martin Luther King, the Baptist minister, who was one of the leaders of the civil rights movement in the USA until his assassination earlier that same year, believed that as Christians we must stand up for what we know to be right according to God's Word, and protest peacefully against all that is evil and wrong in the world. It is certainly true that all it takes for evil to win the day is for good people to do nothing.

Paul exhorts us with these words: '… take your stand against the devil's schemes … put on the full armour of God, so that when the day of evil comes, you may be able to stand your ground, and after you have done everything, to stand' [Ephesians 6:11,13]. It seems to me that on many occasions down the years we, as Christians, have not taken our stand and done everything we could to seek to stem the tide of evil that continues to rise in the world. There are several notable exceptions to this, both people and organisations who have been in the vanguard of protest and action, and we should praise God for them.

Such protest often comes at a cost, as Smith and Carlos found out; but the cost of allowing evil to triumph is surely far greater. The question is: Are we prepared to raise a clenched fist in the face of the devil and his schemes in the name of Jesus, who paid the ultimate cost to deliver us from evil?

Prayer

Thank you, Father God, that you have given us your armour with which to fight against the enemy.

I ask you to bless, strengthen and protect all those who are involved in different forms of peaceful protest and action against all that is evil in the world.

May I, too, be prepared to play my part in standing against the devil's schemes.

Amen.

POWER BOOST

Have you ever wondered how the steeplechase got its name? Apparently, it's because this type of race was first run from the church steeple in one village to the church steeple in the next village. Whether such races always included obstacles is open to debate. In today's steeplechase events the athletes have to run 3,000 metres, negotiating 28 hurdles and seven water jumps on the way.

Percy Hodge of Great Britain was a superb exponent of this event. He won the gold medal by a margin of 100 metres at the 1920 Games in Antwerp, setting a new Olympic record in the process. He was such a top class hurdler that he used to give exhibitions of the art, clearing hurdles while carrying a tray, a bottle and glasses filled to the brim, without spilling a single drop!

Running the 5,000 and 10,000 metres demands even more endurance of the athlete than the steeplechase. To win one of these events is daunting enough, but to win both at the same Olympics is a phenomenal achievement. Unbelievably, Lasse Viren, a policeman from Finland, did this not once, but twice: at the 1972 Games in Munich and at the 1976 Games in Montreal. What he accomplished in Munich is particularly amazing, given that he set a new world record in the 10,000 metres, having fallen over halfway through the race, and then went on to break the Olympic record in the 5,000 metres!

Interestingly, Viren took little part in athletics meetings between the Olympics and the times he recorded at the Games were far better than anything else he ever did.

This led to accusations that he was indulging in the practice of blood boosting, a perfectly legal procedure at the time, which had first been developed in Scandinavia. About a quart of blood would be taken from the athlete at a point in his training which would allow enough time for his body to get its blood back to the normal level before the competition. That quart of blood would be frozen, then unfrozen in time to be re-injected into the athlete just before the race. The effect of this was to increase the body's haemoglobin level and oxygen-carrying capability, thus providing the athlete with greater endurance.

Viren consistently denied such accusations, maintaining that his phenomenal success was all down to his training schedule, designed so that he was in peak condition for the Olympics.

Endurance is a constant theme throughout the writings of Paul. He himself had to endure many sufferings and hardships for the sake of the Gospel, and he exhorts us also to 'endure hardship', in whatever form it may come [2 Corinthians 6:4-10; 2 Timothy 4:5]. If my experience is anything to go by, life is rather like a steeplechase course, presenting us almost daily with different obstacles to overcome, which test our endurance to the limit. There are times when I feel like giving up and just sitting down on the track in despair.

But it's at times like these that God's Word encourages me to get up and go on. Paul makes it very clear that God doesn't expect us to endure in our own strength. God knows the race that we run, and the obstacles that we face, and how difficult we find it to keep going at times. So Paul tells the Colossians that they are 'being strengthened with all power according to his glorious might so that you may have great endurance…' [1:11]. God's Holy Spirit provides us with all the boosting we need to enable us to endure, which is why Paul exhorts us to be filled with the Spirit [Ephesians 5:18]. Thus empowered, we can overcome those obstacles which lie in our path as we 'press on towards the goal to win the prize…' [Philippians 3:14].

The members of the church at Ephesus received this ringing endorsement from the Lord Jesus himself: 'You have persevered and have endured hardships for my name, and have not grown weary' [Revelation 2:3]. May we seek to be worthy of having the same accolade bestowed on us.

Prayer

Father God, you know all about the obstacles I face, and how hard I find it to overcome them at times.

Please strengthen me by the power of your Spirit so that I may endure to the end, and not grow weary.

I pray especially for all those who are struggling today, that they may find encouragement in your Word, and know the empowering of your Spirit.

Amen.

Jessie Owens takes part in the long jump in the 1936 Berlin Olympics – see pages 18-19, 52-53.

Eric Liddell running 1924 – see pages 7, 10-11.

Tommie Smith and John Carlos give the Black Power salute on the podium in Mexico 1968 – see page 26.

Derek Redmond struggles home, injured and supported by his father, in the 1992 Olympics at Barcelona – see page 34.

RUNNING ALONGSIDE

The greatest endurance race of the Olympics is undoubtedly the marathon. It recreates the legend of Philippides, who allegedly brought to Athens the news of the Greek victory over the Persians at the battle of Marathon in 490 BC. The distance he ran was 26 miles; but at the 1908 Games held in London, 385 yards were added so that the race would finish directly in front of the royal box where Queen Alexandra was sitting! This eventually became the official length of the marathon.

One of the greatest runners ever to compete in the marathon was Emil Zatopek. A carpenter's son from Koprivnice in Czechoslovakia, he was one of the most amazing and popular athletes ever to compete at the Olympics. Between 1948 and 1954, he won 38 consecutive races at 10,000 metres and, when he came to the 1952 Games in Helsinki, he was probably at the peak of his career. His running style caused much comment, as his face always looked contorted with pain, while his shoulders and body were hunched, giving the impression that he was in great distress. When he was asked about this, he simply said, "I was not talented enough to run and smile at the same time"!

Zatopek had burst onto the scene at the 1948 London Games, where he won gold in the 10,000 metres and silver in the 5,000. Now, four years later, he eclipsed that achievement by winning gold in both those events. But then Zatopek caused a sensation by deciding to enter the marathon, an event in which he had never run before, a fact that did not concern him unduly. If he won, he would achieve an unprecedented treble of gold medals.

He was confident that he had the necessary endurance to complete the course, but he was slightly concerned about the best strategy for running the race. Knowing that Jim Peters of Great Britain, the world record holder at this distance, was the favourite to win, he decided to run alongside him. Peters set off at a very fast pace, but Zatopek kept up with him.

Approaching the halfway point, Zatopek turned to Peters and said to him, in English, "The pace? Is it good enough?" Peters, who was exhausted from setting off so fast, wanted to pretend that he was still fresh, so he replied, "Pace too slow." Zatopek looked puzzled and asked Peters if he was sure about this. When Peters replied that he was, Zatopek thought for a short while and then sprinted off into the distance. He won in a new Olympic record time and was already signing autographs by the time the second-placed runner entered the stadium. Peters finished well down the field.

It must have been very discouraging to run in the same event as Zatopek; not just because you knew who was going to win before you started, but because he never seemed to have any problems at all during the race. Everything appeared to go so smoothly for him. I wouldn't be at all surprised if the other athletes were thinking, 'It's not fair! Why doesn't he suffer like I do!'

In the same way, it's so easy for us to get discouraged and even to become embittered when we look around at others who don't seem to have anything like the same kind of problems that we do. Maybe there are times when we feel like crying out to God about the apparent unfairness of it all. In such times of distress it is easy to forget that Jesus, not others, should be our focus [Hebrews 12:2] and that he is actually running alongside us, our 'ever present help in trouble' [Psalm 46:1]. He is right there, ready to pick us up when we fall, to lift us up when we are bowed down, to bind up our hearts when they are broken, to tend us when we are wounded and to set us on our way with renewed strength, and with hearts full of gladness and praise [Psalm 145:14; 147:3; Isaiah 40:31; 61:3]. Indeed, it is often when we are in the *deepest distress* that we experience God in the *deepest measure*. And he always knows what the best strategy is!

Paul knew what it was to suffer and, when he sought God on the matter, he was told, 'My grace is sufficient for you, for my power is made perfect in weakness.' This revelation changed Paul's way of looking at things. 'Therefore,' he wrote, 'I will boast all the more gladly about my weaknesses, so that Christ's power may rest on me. That is why, for Christ's sake, I delight in weaknesses, in insults, in hardships, in persecutions, in difficulties. For when I am weak, then I am strong' [2 Corinthians 12:9-10].

Prayer

Thank you, Lord Jesus, that you are running alongside me.

Thank you that you are with me today to minister to me, whatever my need may be.

Help me always to have the right attitude when problems come my way, seeing them as an opportunity to experience more of your power and grace in my life.

Amen.

I'VE STARTED, SO HELP ME FINISH!

As Derek Redmond of Great Britain took his place in lane five for the start of the 400 metres semi-final at the 1992 Games in Barcelona, he thought of all the time, money and care his father had given to help him through the catalogue of injuries he had battled against over the past few years. Back at the 1988 Games in Seoul, Redmond had experienced the heartbreak of having to withdraw from his heat just a few minutes before it was due to take place. Since then, he had undergone five operations, mostly on his Achilles tendon; but here he was, at last, feeling fit and running well, with every chance of making an Olympic final.

He got a good start and all was going well; then 150 metres into the race, disaster struck. Redmond heard a 'pop'; he had torn his right hamstring. He collapsed onto the track in pain; his race was over, his Olympic dream shattered. Stretcher-bearers rushed to his aid, but he was determined not to be carried out of the arena; he desperately wanted to complete the race. So, staying in his lane, he hopped and hobbled his way towards the finish.

Redmond's father, Jim, saw the tragedy unfold from the stand. Seeing his son in so much pain, he could sit there no longer. He rushed out of the stand and onto the track, by which time Redmond was hobbling round the bottom bend. Jim ran to meet him and said, "You don't have to do this". "I've got to finish," came the reply. "Okay," said Jim. "We started your career together, so we're going to finish this race together." At that, Jim put an arm around his son's shoulder, held his hand and together they set off towards the finish *(see photo on page 31)*. Son leant against father and sobbed. As they approached the finish, Jim let go of his son so he could take the last few steps on his own. The crowd of 65,000 people stood to applaud Redmond home.

What a moving scene that must have been to witness! Father and son together there on the track; the one who had encouraged him through many difficulties and discouragements in the past now walking with him, an arm round his shoulder, helping him to finish the race. What a lovely picture this is of the ministry of encouragement! In my experience, this is one of the most important ministries in the church, and one in which we are all involved. Paul makes this clear when he exhorts us to 'encourage one another and build each other up' [1 Thessalonians 5:11].

Barnabas is a fine example of this ministry in action. His actual name was Joseph, but the encouragement and support that he gave to others had such an impact on the church that the apostles themselves gave him the name Barnabas, which means 'Son of Encouragement' [Acts 4:36]. The book of Acts also tells us that it was Barnabas who welcomed the newly converted Saul into the church at Jerusalem, when all the others wouldn't go near him [9:27]. It was Barnabas who encouraged the newly established church in Antioch, and who was always prepared to give people a second chance, despite the consequences [11:22-23; 15:36-39].

Derek Redmond benefited greatly from the support and encouragement of his family. We too have the privilege of ministering in this way, not only to our natural family, but also to the family of God. And who knows where our encouragement may lead! I'm sure Barnabas had no idea that the man he had 'put his arm round' would one day become the apostle Paul! Nor did Geoff Clarke, a Sunday School teacher, realise the impact his encouragement would have on swimmer Adrian Moorhouse, who had once been in his class. Mr Clarke sent the swimmer a telegram after he finished a disappointing fourth in the 100 metres breaststroke at the 1984 Games. It read: 'Very bad luck, all proud of you. There will be a next time.' Moorhouse kept this telegram and took it with him to the 1988 Games in Seoul. When he won the gold in the 100 metres breaststroke, he put the telegram into the box with the medal.

Prayer

Father God, thank you for the privilege I have of encouraging and supporting others.

Help me to be aware of what is happening to those around me, and to be sensitive as I seek to support them.

Thank you for those who have encouraged me in the past. Help me to encourage others in a similar way.

Amen.

Whatever form our encouragement may take, be it an arm round the shoulder, a word spoken at the right time, or some other way, may we always be aware of what is happening to others around us, and seek to support and encourage one another daily [Hebrews 3:13].

IN PERSPECTIVE

Mention the 1972 Munich Games and most people think of the tragic events which occurred there on 5th September. That was the day when eight Palestinian terrorists broke into the Olympic village, killed two Israeli athletes and took nine hostage *(see photo on page 57)*. In the end, all the hostages were killed, along with five of the terrorists.

When the Games eventually resumed, one of the events that took place was the basketball final between the USA and the Soviet Union. The Americans were hot favourites, but lost the match in controversial circumstances. Kenny Davis was a member of the American team but, unlike some of his team-mates, he was able to keep their defeat in perspective. Speaking about what happened, he said, "I went back to my room and cried alone that night. But every time I get to feeling sorry for myself, I think of the Israeli kids who were killed at those Games…Think of being in a helicopter with your hands tied behind your back and a hand grenade rolling towards you…and compare *that* to not getting a gold medal."

If my experience is anything to go by, it's so easy to let things get out of perspective in our lives. Problems and worries often assume a significance of gargantuan proportions; a significance which is entirely unwarranted. This usually happens because our perception of the situation has been distorted by the mixture of powerful emotions that we feel. So it's no wonder that our perspective is affected.

The Psalmists, especially King David, sometimes found themselves in danger of getting things out of perspective. On such occasions, they would remind themselves that God is almighty and all powerful and can deal with any situation; then they would affirm their faith and trust in God, asking him to strengthen them and guide them. This helped to restore a true perspective, and brought peace to their souls, even in the midst of turmoil. And the God of David is our God too! He can and will do the same for us as we seek him in prayer.

Jonathan Edwards of Great Britain and Haile Gebrselassie of Ethiopia, gold medal winners at the 2000 Games in the triple jump and the 10,000 metres respectively, certainly kept their success in its true perspective. When he was asked what his biggest wish was at that moment of triumph, Edwards replied, "To be at home with my wife. Alison and the boys are the most important part of my life." *(See photo on page 56.)* Gebrselassie let it be known that he would not be taking his medal home. "I will give my gold medal to the church; there is no place like it," he said. It would hang there alongside the gold medal he had previously won in the 10,000 metres at the 1996 Games. Two special gifts to honour God.

At those same Games in Atlanta, Noureddine Morceli of Algeria won the gold in the 1500 metres. Later, he spoke to the press. His words certainly put success at the Olympics into perspective. Morceli told the assembled media, "The records and medals are wonderful, but they are mere trinkets in reality. They cannot feed all the people in the world who are hungry, clothe all those who are cold, comfort all those who are troubled, or bring peace to all those who are at war. That is a race we must all run together."

In the parable of the sheep and the goats [Matthew 25:31-46], we see what God's perspective is, and what is important in his eyes. Jesus makes it clear in this parable that we will all be called to account for the way we have responded in service to our fellow-man. We will not be asked what medals we have won or what our personal achievements have been. Rather, we will be judged on our ministry to the needy. Not that our salvation depends on works; but according to the parable, God expects to see us doing good works as the outcome of our salvation. Paul makes this clear in his letter to the Ephesians [2:8-10].

Paul Anderson, a devout Christian, won a weightlifting gold medal at the 1956 Melbourne Games. But far more important to him was running a home for delinquent and orphaned children back home in the United States. He had things in perspective; God's perspective.

Prayer

Father God, please help me to keep what happens in my life in perspective.

I praise you that you are the almighty one in whom I can put my trust.

Please strengthen me, guide me, and give me your peace.

I pray especially for all those across the world who are suffering or are in need in any way. Bless those who seek to minister to them today.

Help me also to play my part, and to do it all as for you.

Amen.

BOTTLED

Joseph Guillemot was a rather unlikely Olympic athlete. The Frenchman was only 5 feet 3 inches tall, his heart was on the right-hand side of his chest, and he smoked a packet of cigarettes a day! Yet, he took part in the 1920 Games at Antwerp with distinction. In the 5,000 metres final, he was up against Paavo Nurmi, the unsmiling runner from Finland, who had already beaten him into second place in the 10,000 metres. Nurmi would prove to be one of the great Olympic athletes, winning a total of four gold and two silver medals at the 1920, 1924 and 1928 Games.

Guillemot was out for revenge. Before the race, Guillemot's coach gave him a mysterious concoction to drink, saying, "Swallow this and you will be unbeatable." With 200 metres to go, Nurmi was in front, with Guillemot on his shoulder. Then Guillemot put in a sprint and won by 20 metres. As for the mysterious concoction: it turned out to be water, with some sugar and rum mixed in!

Another Frenchman, Georges André, was a finalist in the high jump at the 1908 Games held in London. In 1922, he gave an interview in which he talked about something that had happened during that high jump final back in 1908. André had noticed that from time to time the coaches of the United States team were giving their jumpers something to drink from blue coloured bottles, which they kept hidden away. He became convinced that this mysterious liquid was assisting the performance of the Americans, a notion apparently confirmed when one of them, Harry Porter, won the event with a jump that broke the Olympic record. André had to be content with the silver medal.

Taking stimulants was not illegal in those days; drug testing had not yet been introduced. André was intrigued to find out whether this liquid would improve his own performance, so he decided to steal one of the blue bottles when the event was over. Having managed this successfully, he made his way back to the changing room, only to be confronted by one of the American coaches. André thought he must have been spotted, but the coach only wanted to congratulate him on his silver medal. In the privacy of his room, André examined the blue bottle closely. Stuck on the outside was a label bearing the legend 'Sun Water'.

During his next competition, André took surreptitious sips from the blue bottle, but there was no improvement in his performance. In the end, he could contain his curiosity no longer and had the mysterious liquid analysed. The secret was at last revealed; the blue bottle contained…water!

The growth in the bottled water industry only serves to emphasise how important this liquid is for our survival, and how precious it is – a fact that is easily forgotten in countries where it's readily available. But, as Jesus said to the Samaritan woman at the well, 'Everyone who drinks this water will be thirsty again…' [John 4:13]. He then went on to explain the difference between this water from the well and the water that he himself has provided for us to drink, saying, 'but whoever drinks the water I give him will never thirst. Indeed, the water I give him will become in him a spring of water welling up to eternal life' [John 4:14].

We live in a thirsty world, which seeks to quench its cravings at wells of its own making. The water found here may satisfy for a time, but it can never fulfil our deepest longings or meet our deepest needs, no matter how often or in what form it is drunk. Only God's precious, living water can do that [Psalm 107:8-9].

It is also a proven fact that, if we don't drink water that is pure and clean, we will suffer from all manner of sickness and disease as a result. Every day the newspapers and the television show us very clearly what a sick society we live in. The only cure for this sickness, which is caused by sin, is God's pure and purifying water, drawn from the well of salvation [Isaiah 12:3].

How we should thank God for his Word – his pure, precious, living water, bottled for distribution to the world!

Prayer

Father God, I thank you that the pure, precious, living water of your Word is freely available to everyone.

I praise you for the day I first drank from it, and found that you had provided for my salvation and for my every need.

Strengthen me as I seek to make your living water known to others.

Please bless and keep all those who are involved in distributing your Word throughout the world.

Amen.

TRIAL BY TRIALS

One of the eight women sprinters lining up for the final of the 100 metres at the 1992 Games in Barcelona was Gail Devers of the USA. The fact that she had made it to the Games at all was quite amazing, considering all the trials she had been through during the previous four years. It was back in June 1988 that she first started getting bad migraine headaches, accompanied by dizziness and loss of sight in one eye for a time. She was eventually diagnosed as having Graves disease.

This meant that she had to undergo radiation therapy to control her hyperactive thyroid. This treatment began in September 1990 and was very successful. Unfortunately, however, she reacted extremely badly to the radiation. She haemorrhaged blood clots, her weight fluctuated dramatically, and she experienced second-degree burns on her feet, which became infected and swollen.

All this meant that she missed out on over two years of training, yet here she was, about to take part in one of the closest 100 metres finals ever to take place at the Olympics. There was a blanket finish but in the end Devers, who had run a personal best time, was awarded the gold medal. She would have made it a double gold triumph had she not hit the last hurdle and lost her balance when in the lead in the final of the 100 metre hurdles.

Most, if not all, athletes experience setbacks during their careers, and there are many examples of perseverance, determination, courage and fortitude shown in the face of such trials. British javelin thrower Fatima Whitbread won the silver medal at the 1988 Seoul Games, despite having suffered the following setbacks during the twelve months leading up to the Games: a trapped nerve in her throwing shoulder, a foot injury, a mouth infection, an abscess in her back, hamstring problems, glandular fever and a car crash.

Other athletes have been so determined to compete that they have not even allowed the loss of limbs to deter them! American gymnast George Eyser had his left leg amputated and replaced with a wooden one after he was run over by a train. Yet he still went on to win gold in the long horse vault, two silvers in the pommel horse and combined competitions, and bronze in the horizontal bar at the 1904 Games! And what about Károly Takács, who had his right hand completely shattered while serving in the army when a grenade he was holding exploded? Undaunted, the Hungarian taught himself to shoot with his left hand, and won a gold medal at the 1948 Games in the rapid-fire pistol event with a world record score!

The writer of the letter to the Hebrews exhorts us to 'run with perseverance the race marked out for us' [Hebrews 12:1]. This indicates that each one of us has a different race to run and each will have its own particular problems, difficulties and setbacks. Just as the athletes mentioned found, the going will get tough at times for all of us. It is very challenging to consider how we respond when faced with such trials in our lives.

It is so easy to give up, to grow weary and to lose heart, and I know I have been guilty of this at times. But God's Word encourages us to show perseverance and determination, taking our example from Jesus himself, 'who for the joy set before him endured the cross' [Hebrews 12:2]. Indeed, James begins his letter by exhorting us to 'Consider it pure joy' when we face 'trials of many kinds', rather than being dismayed! He points out that trials test our faith, and this testing 'develops perseverance', which will bring us to maturity as Christians [James 1:2-4]. He goes on to say, 'Blessed is the man who perseveres under trial, because when he has stood the test, he will receive the crown of life that God has promised to those who love him' [1:12]. What an encouragement that is to each one of us!

John Akhwari, a marathon runner from Tanzania competing in the 1968 Games, entered the stadium in Mexico City well over an hour after the winner of the event. He had fallen during the race, injuring his knee and now staggered towards the finish, bloodied and bandaged. Later he was asked why he hadn't dropped out, given the obvious pain that he was in. Akhwari replied, "My country did not send me 7,000 miles away to start the race. They sent me 7,000 miles to finish it."

This example of amazing perseverance reminds me of Paul's words, which come as an inspiration to us all: 'I consider my life worth nothing to me, if only I may finish the race and complete the task the Lord Jesus has given me…' [Acts 20:24].

Prayer

Father God, I confess that there are times when the problems I face make me feel weary and cause me to lose heart, until I feel like giving up.

Please strengthen me so that when trials test my faith, I may persevere, grow in spiritual maturity, and finish the race you have marked out for me.

Amen.

A BEAUTIFUL IDEA

Marty Glickman of the USA stood in the Olympic stadium in Berlin and looked around him. In his mind's eye he could see and hear the crowd and sense that special atmosphere once again. Over the far side of the stadium, he could see the place from which Adolf Hitler and his entourage had watched the Games and the enclosure reserved for the athletes. It all came flooding back as Glickman, now 68 years of age, relived what had happened at the 1936 Games. He was only 18 years old back then, but he was in the 4 x 100-relay team, the favourites for the gold medal.

There was speculation about whether Jesse Owens would be added to the relay squad after his gold medal runs in the 100 and 200 metres. However, the team coach, Lawson Robertson, told the press that Glickman, Stoller and Wykoff were definite starters, and the final place in the relay would be between Draper and Metcalfe. "Owens," he said, "has had enough glory and collected enough gold medals to last him a while." But then, on the morning of the heats, Glickman and Stoller were taken to one side by the coaches and told that they were being dropped from the team in favour of Metcalfe and…you've guessed it…Owens.

The reason Robertson gave was that he was concerned about the speed of the Dutch and German teams, so he wanted his four fastest runners in the relay. But it wasn't as simple as that. What made the decision particularly distasteful was the fact that both Glickman and Stoller were Jews. In fact, they were the only Jews in the whole US team and were the only athletes in that team who didn't compete at all in the Games. Glickman always blamed Avery Brundage, the President of the US Olympic Committee, for the decision. It was Glickman's firm belief that Brundage had withdrawn the two Jews from the relay to avoid the possibility of humiliating Hitler. In the event, the US quartet won easily in a new world record time, while Glickman and Stoller watched from the athletes enclosure.

Reliving all these painful memories, Glickman walked across the stadium and stood at the very spot on the track where he should have taken his mark to run his leg of the relay. He told the *New York Times* what happened as he stood there: "Suddenly, a wave of rage overwhelmed me. I thought I was going to pass out. I began to scream every dirty curse word, every obscenity I knew. How could you no-good, dirty so-and-sos do this

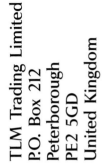

The Leprosy Mission International

The Leprosy Mission (TLM) is an international Christian charity caring for people affected by leprosy. TLM was founded in 1874 by Irishman Wellesley Bailey. It is motivated and inspired by Christ's ministry of compassion to people suffering from leprosy. Today TLM is working in 28 countries, treating almost 300,000 people personally affected by leprosy.

TLM aims to meet the physical, mental, social and spiritual needs of people affected by leprosy, whilst working towards the eventual eradication of the disease. The Mission has over 2,000 field staff and works both directly, through its own hospitals and programmes, and in partnership with churches, voluntary agencies, patient organisations, governments and international organisations to meet the broad-ranging needs of people affected by leprosy. It is supported by voluntary contributions of churches, support groups and individuals around the world and has an international budget of over £12 million.

Leprosy is a medical condition affecting millions of people, 90% of whom live in the developing world. If left untreated, it causes disability and even blindness. It is not hereditary but is caused by a bacillus which attacks the nerves under the skin causing inflammation and anaesthesia. It is not a punishment for sin! Over 95% of the world's population is naturally immune and, after only a few days of treatment with Multidrug therapy (MDT), patients are no longer infectious. Since the 1980s over 10 million people have been cured with MDT, but the challenge remains as over 750,000 new cases are still detected each year.

TLM Trading is a wholly owned subsidiary of The Leprosy Mission and raises funds for TLM's work through selling a wide variety of books, gifts, stationery and craftware made by leprosy affected people to create employment and help restore dignity.

TLM Trading Limited
P.O. Box 212
Peterborough
PE2 5GD
United Kingdom

Please use your local Leprosy Mission address if you prefer, see page 80

Please affix stamp

The Leprosy Mission Response Card

The Olympics of Life is Ray Markham's fourth book. His earlier titles, published by Autumn House, are all now available from TLM Trading Limited. The sale of all books from the TLM catalogue helps to raise funds for people affected by leprosy. Please send in this enquiry form if you are interested in purchasing any of the following titles, or if you would like a complete catalogue.

Titles by Ray Markham	Order Code
Pointed and Personal (*on the parables of Jesus*)	03954
What Kind of Power is This? (*on the miracles of Jesus*)	03040
Greater Expectations (*on the Sermon on the Mount*)	03955
The Olympics of Life	03200

Recent titles by Eddie Askew	
Love is a Wild Bird	03103
Love is a Wild Bird (*audio cassette*)	20202
Talking with Hedgehogs	03028
Talking with Hedgehogs (*audio cassette*)	20201
Unexpected Journeys	03100

We can also offer you two delightful children's books.

Garth the Giraffe by Brian Ogden.
A collection of twelve short stories for 4-7 year olds on themes like the importance of friends, listening and sharing. 03560

The Wonderful Picnic by Hilary Faith Jones.
This is a charming colour storybook for younger children. We are sure that you will enjoy reading about Minimus Mouse and his best friend, Jesus the Carpenter. 03301

Please send me information about:- (please tick)

☐ The Leprosy Mission's mail-order catalogue

☐ The Leprosy Mission's work

☐ Prayer support

☐ Sending a regular gift by automatic payment, standing order, or direct debit to support The Leprosy Mission

☐ Tax efficient ways of supporting The Leprosy Mission

☐ Service Overseas with The Leprosy Mission

☐ Making and amending a Will and leaving a legacy to The Leprosy Mission

Credit card sales and enquiries:
Tel: 0845 1662253   Fax: 01733 239258
E-mail address: enquiries@tlmtrading.com

Title .... Initials .... Surname ....

Address...

.... Post Code.................. Country..................

Source code: TLMT 244

to an 18-year-old kid, to any young man who worked so hard to get there? …For 49 years that anger and frustration, that rage, had been inside me… But being there, visualising and reliving those moments, caused the eruption which had been gnawing at me for so long, and which I thought I had expunged years ago."

In his letter to the Ephesians, Paul wrote these uncompromising words: 'Get rid of all bitterness, rage and anger…forgiving each other, just as in Christ God forgave you' [Ephesians 4:31-32]. Paul is pointing out that the only way to get rid of these destructive emotions, which eat us up inside, is to forgive. And our forgiveness is to be like Christ's forgiveness: genuine and unconditional.

If my experience is anything to go by, forgiving others is far from easy. It's hard to forgive when we've been hurt. As C S Lewis said: "We all agree that forgiveness is a beautiful idea, until we have to practise it." Forgiveness is an act of the will, not of the emotions. Feelings don't enter into it. If we were to wait until we felt like forgiving somebody, I doubt we ever would.

Why is God so insistent that we forgive? Simply because he loves us, and knows that forgiveness is essential for our welfare, our growth, and our spiritual progress. That is why Jesus warns us so strongly about the consequences of unforgiveness in the parable of the unforgiving servant [Matthew 18:21-35]. He even requires us to forgive others if we want God to forgive us [Luke 11:4]. Of course, this doesn't mean that God won't forgive us until we forgive others, because we know that salvation is the gift of God [Ephesians 2: 8-9]. Rather, it speaks of an attitude that we are required to live in and to show daily. A forgiving spirit is a major evidence of true repentance.

> **Prayer**
>
> *Father God, forgive me for the times when I have harboured bitterness, resentment and anger in my heart.*
>
> *Help me to rid myself of such feelings, and to extend forgiveness to anyone who has wronged me.*
>
> *Thank you most of all for your forgiveness, freely given to me. Amen.*

Forgiveness brings release to the soul. As someone once said: "To forgive is to set a prisoner free, and to discover that the prisoner was you."

PERFECT LOSERS

John Thomas of the USA went to the 1960 Games in Rome as the favourite to win gold in the high jump. The 6-feet 5-inch teenager was the world record holder, had cleared seven feet over 30 times and was undefeated in the past two years. Indeed, the American sportswriters claimed that a gold medal in this event was 'in the bag', because they also had two other top jumpers competing: Charley Dumas, the defending Olympic champion, and Joe Faust, a teenager who had also cleared seven feet. One of these three was certain to win.

In the event, Faust didn't jump well due to an ankle injury and was eliminated; Dumas, who was carrying a knee injury, finished sixth. All American hopes rested on Thomas, who was up against three jumpers from the Soviet Union: Robert Shavlakadze, Valery Brumel and Viktor Bolshov. In a tense finale to the competition, Shavlakadze and Brumel took the gold and silver, and Thomas the bronze.

Naturally, Thomas was disappointed, but he was proud to have won an Olympic medal. The American sportswriters, however, were anything but proud of him and his achievement. Having built him up in the run-up to the 1960 Games, they now tore him apart, calling him, amongst other things, a quitter and a man with no heart.

Thomas was devastated by their treatment of him and was hurt by the reaction of the fans back home. Brumel, who was invited to take part in a series of competitions in the USA, was shocked by how the crowds treated Thomas. They booed him whenever he missed a jump and whenever he didn't actually win the competition. Coming second was just not acceptable. In their eyes, Thomas was a failure, worthy only of disdain.

It took him a long time to come to terms with all this. Reflecting on the response to his perceived failure in Rome, Thomas said, "That was the first time I learned people didn't like me. They only like winners. In the champion they see what they'd like to be. In the loser they see what they actually are, and they treat him with scorn."

But we can rejoice that this is not the way that God treats us, even though we actually are all losers and failures in his sight. We have all lost our way, and failed to live up to God's holy standard of perfection. Isaiah says that, 'We all, like sheep, have gone astray, each of us has turned to his own way' [Isaiah 53:6], while Paul tells us that 'all have sinned and fall short of the glory of God…' [Romans 3:23].

But these statements do not end there; they both proceed to a wonderful truth. Isaiah continues: 'and the Lord has laid on him the iniquity of us all' [53:6], which means that our sin has been placed on Jesus and he has paid the penalty for it. Because of this, Paul can go on to say that we 'are justified freely by his grace through the redemption that came by Christ Jesus' [Romans 3:24]. When we repent, God forgives us and cleanses us, and restores our relationship with him. Not only that, but he forgets the wrong we have done; indeed it's just as if we'd never sinned [Isaiah 43:25]. God responds to our failure, not by pouring his scorn upon us, but by pouring his grace upon us; not by rejecting us out of hand, but by extending to us the hand of mercy; not by keeping us at arms' length, but by enfolding us in arms of love. Paul has more to say about the wonder of this love for losers: 'But God demonstrates his own love for us in this: While we were still sinners, Christ died for us' [Romans 5:8].

At the 1976 Games in Montreal, there was a sensation in the women's gymnastics competition. For the first time in Olympic history, a gymnast had achieved a score of ten – a score only awarded for absolute perfection. That gymnast was Nadia Comaneci of Romania who, according to the judges, had put in a perfect performance on both the asymmetric bars and the beam. Before the competition was over, she had been awarded the perfect score of ten no less than seven times.

Although none of us is perfect, we have been made perfect through Jesus' sacrifice for us on the cross [Hebrews 10:14]. Because of God's love for losers, we can all be winners in Christ.

Prayer

Father God, I thank you that you have poured out your grace upon me; that you have shown me mercy; that you have enfolded me in your arms of love.

I marvel at the wonder of your love and the greatness of your forgiveness.

I thank you that through the death of Jesus, I have been made perfect to enter into your most holy presence.

Amen.

ALL IMPORTANT

Officer Al Stankie of the Los Angeles Police Department first came across Paul Gonzales when he was helping to break up yet another street fight in an area of the city notorious for its gang warfare. A 'ghetto's ghetto' is how Gonzales himself described it. It was there that he and his seven brothers and sisters were brought up by their mother. Their father had left them when he was only seven years old. And here he was, at the age of ten, fighting for his life in the street.

Officer Stankie was very impressed by this young fighter and persuaded him to take up boxing. Stankie was a boxing coach and the gym he used was in the basement of the police station. This posed a bit of a problem for Gonzales. He didn't want the members of his gang to think he was a 'grass' or a 'snitch', so he used to climb into the gym through a window at the back. He still went out with the gang. When he was 12, he was shot in the side of the head. In keeping with gang procedures, he went to a nearby park, washed his head in the lake and then got his cousin to take out the remaining pieces of shot with some tweezers!

As he grew older, it became obvious that Gonzales had a real talent for boxing, so he went into serious training. To the derision of his mates, he stopped drinking, went to bed early and got up at five in the morning to go running. However, as he achieved success as a boxer, they got behind him and made sure he didn't let up on his training. Gonzales boxed in the light flyweight class and, when he was 18, he faced Shamil Sabirov of the Soviet Union, the Olympic champion. He caused a sensation by beating the Russian, thus raising the hopes of all his supporters that he might win a gold medal at the forthcoming 1984 Olympics.

Funnily enough, these Games were due to be held in his home city of Los Angeles. In fact, the boxing ring was only four miles from where he lived in the Aliso Village housing project! The pressure on him from his wild and enthusiastic supporters was huge, but he managed to block it out and fought his way to the final. His performances were so impressive that he won the Val Barker award for the best boxer at the Olympics.

The final was a complete anti-climax, as his opponent, Salvatore Todisco of Italy, had broken a thumb in his semi-final bout and arrived with his hand in a cast. Gonzales was awarded the gold medal. He said later, "I won this gold medal, not just for myself or my mom or my coach, but for the kids like me who are always told, 'You're nothing.'"

The Pharisees of Jesus' day would have called such kids 'sinners'. Indeed, that was the word they used to describe anyone who broke God's law. They considered such people to be rejects in God's eyes; they were nothing; they had no value; they were unimportant. So the Pharisees just couldn't cope with the fact that Jesus welcomed such people and even ate with them [Luke 15:1-2]. Such an action meant that he was accepting them and recognising them as people of value and importance. The Pharisees had got it so completely wrong; nobody is nothing in God's sight. Though we are all sinners, we still matter to God; we are all equally valuable and important to him.

To emphasise this truth, Jesus told the parables of the lost sheep and the lost coin [Luke 15:3-10]. In each case, the owners take the initiative to find what they have lost. Both items are of such great value to their owners that they are totally focused on finding them. The sheep and the coin are of such great value, and are so important to them, that they continue to search, despite all the difficulties and problems which they encounter, until they eventually succeed in finding them. And when they do, the extent of their rejoicing shows the value and importance to them of what they have found.

Unlike other religions, where man is desperately searching for God, the Christian faith is underpinned by the glorious truth that God loves us so much that he himself took the initiative, came searching for us and sacrificed himself for us. That's how precious and valuable we are to him. May we always rejoice and revel in the wonder of this all-important truth: we are all important to God.

Prayer

Father God, thank you for seeking me, finding me, and drawing me to yourself.

I rejoice in your love for me, and marvel at how valuable and important I am to you.

Help me always to see everyone I meet in the same way as you see them.

Amen.

WITH A DIFFERENCE

The crowd watching the high jump competition at the 1968 Games in Mexico City could not believe its eyes. One of the competitors had just done something never seen before at a high jump event. There were gasps of disbelief, followed by a buzz of excited conversation. In fact, what they had all just witnessed was nothing less than a revolution in the technique of clearing the bar. The high jump would never be the same again. And the name of the athlete who had introduced this innovative technique? – Dick Fosbury of the United States.

Jumpers used to take off from their inside foot and swing their outside foot over the bar. What Fosbury did was run towards the bar and, as he neared it, took off from his outside foot, turned his back to the bar and jumped over it both backwards and head first! He won the gold with an Olympic record jump. His technique was soon dubbed 'the Fosbury flop' and it took the world of high jumping by storm. So much so that, at the 1980 Games in Moscow, 13 of the 16 finalists used the Fosbury flop and now it is rare to see any other technique being employed *(see photo on page 57)*.

And then, at the 1976 Games in Montreal, something just as innovative and revolutionary happened in the gymnastics hall. Mitsuo Tsukahara of Japan came to those Games as the defending champion in the horizontal bar event and once again secured the gold medal. However, it was his technique in another event, the vault, which had everybody talking. He was the first gymnast to perform the vault sideways!

As Tsukahara approached the apparatus, he did a cartwheel, hitting the horse in the middle of the move and springing off it into a backflip. At the time, this way of performing the vault was considered to be incredibly daring, if not downright dangerous! But this innovative technique had a dramatic impact on how to perform the vault and, within a few years, many gymnasts had mastered it. Eventually it became the norm and is now part of the compulsory exercises for women.

Dick Fosbury and Mitsuo Tsukahara did it with a difference and consequently they both made a difference to their events. The Bible tells us that our 'event' is the preaching of the Gospel. Jesus instructed all his disciples to 'Go into all the world and preach the good news…' [Mark 16:15]. Paul's approach to preaching the Gospel is both interesting and instructive. He reveals his strategy in his first letter to the Corinthians. His aim in communicating the good news was 'to win as many as possible'; so, 'to the Jews I became like a Jew, to win the Jews … To those not having the law I became like one not having the law … so as to win those not having the law. To the weak I became weak, to win the weak. I have become all things to all men so that by all possible means I might save some' [1 Corinthians 9:19-22].

It is clear from this passage that Paul was flexible, imaginative, relevant, contemporary, sensitive and innovative in his presentation of the good news. When it came to the all-important event of preaching the Gospel, Paul was certainly prepared to do it with a difference in order to make a difference. The challenging question we have to ask ourselves is: "Are we?"

Perhaps we need to consider prayerfully whether the methods we adopt as churches to communicate the Gospel reflect the principles evident in Paul's approach. Unfortunately, the church seems to have little impact on the lives of the majority of people in the western world today. Yet we have the most powerful, life-changing message of all! It's how to get it across that's often the problem. It seems to me that we need to be constantly reviewing our evangelistic strategies, always looking for new ways to reach people with the Gospel, just as Paul was.

Fosbury and Tsukahara changed the course of high jumping and vaulting. We have the privilege of being involved in an event which can change the course of peoples lives. May God help us to meet the challenges this presents and, in so doing, make a difference to the world.

Prayer

Father God, thank you for the privilege you have given me of being involved in sharing the Gospel with people.

Please give me the strength to play my part in the evangelistic activities organised by my church.

May each church know your boldness, wisdom, inspiration and empowering as they seek to reach out to the community around them.

Amen.

THE PLOUGHMAN'S PRIORITY

Zhu Jianhua of China was the favourite for the high jump gold medal at the 1984 Games in Los Angeles. But it was well known that Zhu had a particular failing; not in his technique, but in his concentration. And this would prove to be his undoing at these Games. While the high jump competition was in progress, the final of the 1500 metres took place on the track. One of the runners was Steve Ovett of Great Britain. He collapsed after the final of the 800 metres, and spent two nights in hospital. However, he recovered sufficiently to make it through to the 1500 metres final.

At the start of the final lap, Ovett was in fourth place. Meanwhile, Zhu was about to make his second attempt to clear 7 feet 7¾ inches, which should have been a formality. As Ovett came round the bend into the back straight, he suddenly felt the severe chest pains he had experienced before. He stepped off the track and collapsed onto the apron of the high jump area. Zhu was stopped from attempting his jump until Ovett had received treatment and been carried away from the area on a stretcher. This took some time and Zhu, who had been much distracted by all that had gone on, decided to pass at this height instead. However, when he re-entered the competition at the next height, he was unable to clear it and had to settle for the bronze medal.

One of the more bizarre examples of how competitors can be distracted happened during the men's hockey event at the 1960 Games in Rome. France were playing Belgium and the French were on the attack. Suddenly, the sound of a whistle was heard and the Belgians stopped playing, thinking the umpire had blown. The French, however, did not stop and hit the ball into the Belgian net for what proved to be the match-winning goal. The whistle had in fact been blown by an Italian policeman on traffic duty just outside the ground where the match was being played!

Weightlifters at the 2000 Games in Sydney got extremely annoyed at the number of times they were distracted by mobile phones ringing. A spokesperson said, "We've had complaints that mobile phones have been going off at crucial moments for the weightlifters, just as they are approaching the weights and their concentration is at its peak." The same thing was happening at the gymnastics events too.

Jesus had some strong words to say on the subject of being distracted: 'No-one who puts his hand to the plough and looks back is fit for service in the kingdom of God' [Luke 9:62]. The ploughman was a familiar sight in the fields in those days and everyone knew what would happen if this worker allowed himself to be distracted from his task: the furrow would not be straight and everyone would be able to see that he had not given his full concentration and commitment to the task he had been given to do.

As disciples of Jesus, we have been given the task of serving God as workers in his kingdom – a task which demands wholehearted commitment and dedication. In the preceding verses [Luke 9:57-61], Jesus has been making this point to various people who wanted to become his disciples. In so doing, he identified certain areas of our lives which can distract us from our main task of serving God. These include our homes, families and the many responsibilities we have. On another occasion, Jesus identified the area of money and possessions [Mark 10:21-22]. None of these are wrong in themselves but, in my experience, they can easily become more important in our lives than the work of the kingdom.

At the 1988 Games, Lawrence Lemieux of Canada was taking part in the Finn class of the sailing events. In the fifth race, he was lying second when he spotted a fellow competitor, Joseph Chan of Singapore, struggling in the water near his capsized boat. Lemieux turned around and rescued Chan. By so doing, he lost all chance of a medal; but he got his priorities right and was given a special award by the International Olympic Committee.

Jesus commands us as his disciples to get our priorities right too. They are to be different from those of the world. Jesus demands that the work of the kingdom has priority in our lives; but this priority comes with a promise [Matthew 6:33].

Prayer

Father God, forgive me for the times I have allowed myself to be distracted from giving the work of your kingdom my full and wholehearted commitment.

Please help me to deal with distractions and to sort out my priorities in a way that is pleasing to you.

I re-dedicate myself to your service today.

Amen.

AROUND THE THRONE

Jesse Owens of the USA was worried. He had only one jump left with which to qualify for the final of the long jump, his best event, having failed with the previous two. As he prepared himself for his final effort, he was approached by one of the other jumpers, Ludwig Long. 'Luz', as he was known, was the archetypal German: tall, blond and blue-eyed. Owens, who was fully aware of the Nazi's views about Negroes and their theory of the 'superiority' of the Aryan race, wondered what this German would say to him.

To his surprise, Long was very friendly and spoke good English. "You should be able to qualify with your eyes closed," he told him, and then suggested that Owens should take off from well behind the board to make sure of his final jump. They continued to talk together and it became apparent that Long didn't go along with the theory of Aryan supremacy at all, although Owens joked that he looked the part.

Owens took Long's advice and just made it through to the final, where the two of them vied for the gold medal. They both broke the Olympic record as the competition reached its climax. Long was roared on by the partisan German crowd packed into the Olympic stadium in Berlin but, in the end, it was Owens who was the victor *(see photo on page 30)*. Long was the first to congratulate him in full view of Hitler.

Their friendship overcame the barriers of racism. Some years later, Owens wrote about the events of 1936, 'You can melt down all the medals and cups I have, and they wouldn't be a plating on the 24-carat friendship I felt for Luz Long at that moment.' Although Long was killed at the battle of St Pietro in July 1943, Owens continued to keep in touch with his family.

The first Games to be held after the War was over took place in London in 1948. One of the competitors in the pole vault was the Reverend Bob Richards of the United States. Known to all as 'The Vaulting Vicar', he won the bronze medal. Four years later in Helsinki, he and his fellow American, Don Laz, fought it out for the gold medal. In the end, the vicar emerged triumphant, vaulting to an Olympic record in the process. He also won the gold medal at the Melbourne Games in 1956, thus becoming the only pole-vaulter to win a total of three Olympic medals.

But that achievement was not all that Bob Richards is remembered for. The Helsinki Games was the first at which the Soviet Union competed and many politicians, journalists and athletes saw the Games as an important propaganda tool in the 'Cold War'. Richards disagreed and did his utmost to promote friendship and interaction between athletes from the Soviet Union and the USA in an effort to break down the barriers between them.

The early church had to come to the realisation that the message of the Gospel was for all people, regardless of their race, colour, nationality, gender, culture, background, status, position or class. Throughout his gospel, Luke emphasises that salvation is for all people, beginning with the message of the angels as they announced the birth of Jesus [Luke 2:10-11]. In his chronicle *The Acts of the Apostles*, Luke records Peter's words: 'I now realise how true it is that God does not show favouritism but accepts men from every nation who fear him and do what is right' [10:34-35].

Paul tells us that the Saviour of all, who was spoken of by Luke, has died for us all [2 Corinthians 5:15]. The Gospel is all-inclusive; no-one is outside of God's grace. All may receive his mercy and experience his love and forgiveness. And when we accept Christ as Saviour, we 'are all sons of God through faith in Christ Jesus…'. This means that in the kingdom of God 'There is neither Jew nor Greek, slave nor free, male nor female, for you are all one in Christ Jesus' [Galatians 3:26, 28]. All are equal in God's sight and are equally welcome in his kingdom.

John's vision, recorded in the book of Revelation, presents us with a wonderful picture. Around the throne of the Lamb of God in heaven is gathered a huge throng of people, praising God for their salvation [5:13; 7:9]. And the striking feature of this throng around the throne is that it is made up of those 'from every tribe and language and people and nation' [5:9].

Prayer

Father God, I thank and praise you that the Gospel is for all people everywhere, whoever they may be, and that includes me.

Help me to see everyone as you see them, and to treat everyone as you treat them.

Amen.

Truly the Gospel knows no barriers and knows no bounds.

NOT MY FAULT!

On the 10th August 1984, the Olympic stadium in Los Angeles was packed with 85,000 people who had come to cheer the nation's heroine home in the 3,000 metres final. That heroine was Mary Decker. She had missed the 1976 Montreal Games due to problems with her legs, and the 1980 Moscow Games because of the United States boycott. On both occasions, she could only sit and watch as athletes she had previously beaten won medals that she felt should have been hers. Between 1981 and 1983, she beat all the top athletes at every distance from 800 to 10,000 metres, setting world records in the mile, the 5,000 metres and the 10,000 metres. Surely the 1984 Games would bring her gold at last.

Originally, she had planned to attempt the 1,500/3,000 metres double, but the scheduling of these events made this difficult. Shortly before the Games began, she withdrew from the 1,500 metres to concentrate fully on the 3,000 metres. Although the main threat to her was more likely to be Maricica Puică of Romania, the press built it up into a confrontation with the South African athlete, Zola Budd. Since she was young, Budd had idolised Decker and kept a poster of her on the bedroom wall. Having qualified to represent Great Britain, as South Africa was barred from the Olympics at that time, Budd was to run against her idol in the final. The stage was set for a dramatic meeting.

Shortly after the halfway point in the race, a group of four athletes broke away from the rest of the field: Budd, Decker, Puică and Wendy Sly of Great Britain. Budd, running barefoot as usual, was in the lead. Then, Decker hit one of Budd's legs, throwing Budd slightly off-balance. A few strides later, they collided again; but this time Decker tripped over Budd's leg, spiking the South African badly, and fell onto the infield, tearing a muscle in her left hip. She was in terrible pain, unable to get up on her own *(see photo on page 57)*. Tears of frustration streamed down Decker's contorted face. Her chance of gold was gone. In fact, she never would win an Olympic medal.

The vast crowd was stunned into silence. When they found their voice, it was to boo Budd for the rest of the race. In the end, Puică won comfortably in an Olympic record time, with Sly second, and a dispirited Budd back in seventh. In the tunnel that led away from the track, a tearful Budd approached Decker saying, "I'm sorry. I'm sorry. I'm sorry." Decker replied, "Don't bother; I don't want to talk to you." Swiss athlete Cornelia Burki, who had been just behind the leading group at the time of the collision, heard Decker's words. She said, "It wasn't Zola's fault, Mary! Not her fault!" "Yes it was," retorted Decker, "I know it was. It was!"

Although we can all appreciate the emotions which gave rise to Mary Decker's uncompromising words, it remains a classic example of someone putting the blame entirely on to someone else when they themselves are equally at fault, as the footage of the race showed. And yet, if we're honest, we are often guilty of this kind of response ourselves. We often try to shift the blame on to someone else, usually with the indignant words: "It's not my fault!" And sometimes it isn't, but most of the time we're just as much to blame as anyone else, and we know it, but we won't admit it!

One of the best examples of this is to be found in the story of Adam and Eve. When God asked Adam if he'd eaten the fruit of the forbidden tree, he blamed Eve for giving him the fruit, and God for putting her there with him in the first place! "It's everybody's fault but mine" is what he was saying. And Eve was no better, because, when God tackled her about the matter, she blamed the serpent! [Genesis 3:12,13].

If my experience is anything to go by, there are times when we find it really hard to admit that we've been wrong. And it's even harder sometimes to say "I'm sorry," especially when the other person, like Mary Decker, is not particularly disposed to forgive. But the great thing about saying sorry to God is that *he* is always ready to forgive, no matter what.

Prayer

Father God, thank you that you are always ready and willing to forgive me, if I am truly repentant.

Forgive me for the times I have blamed other people for what I have done.

Forgive me for the wrongs I have done to others, and for the things I have done that have displeased you.

Give me the strength not to be at fault in those ways again.

Amen.

Kerri Strug, her ankle in a soft cast, is carried by her coach after her gold medal vault – see pages 66-67.

Johnny Weissmuller, in his post-Olympic role as Tarzan – pages 72-73.

Jonathan Edwards in mid flight – pages 36-37.

Palestinian terrorists strike at the Munich Games in 1972 – see page 36.

Mary Decker collides with Zola Budd in 1984 – see pages 54-55.

Dick Fosbury performs the Fosbury flop – see page 48.

TIME OUT!

There were only three seconds left in the 1972 basketball final between the Soviet Union and the USA. Going into these Games held in Munich, the American team were the overwhelming favourites. Indeed, the USA had won every gold medal since basketball was introduced into the Olympic Games in 1936. But they were on the verge of losing, trailing as they did by one point.

Then Sako Sakandelidze of the USSR deliberately fouled Doug Collins and the USA were awarded two free throws. Though dazed, Collins managed to sink both throws, putting the Americans into the lead for the first time in the match by 50 points to 49. What the players didn't realise was that Kondrashkin, the Soviet coach, had called for a 'time-out' after Collins' first shot. A 'time-out' allows a coach to stop the game and discuss tactics with his team before the match has to restart. In fact, the 'time-out' horn went off as Collins was taking his second free throw.

Kondrashkin immediately stormed across to the scorer's table to complain. Meanwhile, the game had re-started, but the head referee stopped it almost immediately, due to the disturbance going on at the scorer's table. There was now just one second left on the clock. The USSR were belatedly awarded their 'time-out' but, when play resumed, they didn't have enough time to score.

But, as the Americans celebrated yet another Olympic triumph, something unprecedented happened. The Secretary-General of the International Amateur Basketball Federation, William Jones of Great Britain, intervened. He ordered that the clock be set back to show three seconds, which was the amount of time remaining when the Soviet coach had originally tried to call a 'time-out'. Even though technically he had no right to make such an intervention, Jones was not a man to be argued with in basketball circles; so back went the clock.

When the Soviet team came back on court, they knew exactly what to do. Kondrashkin had brought on Ivan Edeshko, who threw a long pass to Sasha Belov. Belov caught the ball brilliantly, went past two defenders and scored. At that very moment, the match ended and the USSR had won by

51 points to 50! The crowd went mad. They couldn't believe it any more than the Americans could. In spite of their protest, the result stood. That 'time-out' had changed the whole course of the match.

The gospels tell us that Jesus deliberately took 'time-out' to pray regularly. In fact, Jesus was so busy that he had to make a time to pray and find a place to pray [Matthew 14:23]. He had to organise his life to make sure that communion with his Father didn't get squeezed out of the day, as could so easily have happened.

Although our situations are obviously completely different from that of Jesus, it seems to me that the same principles apply. It is important that somewhere in the routine of each day we call a 'time-out' for the express purpose of spending time with God. And that time can take place anywhere: on the journey to work, going to the shops, while walking the dog, at home, on the bus, in the woods; wherever and whenever. However long or short this 'time-out' might be, it is without doubt the most precious and important time of our day.

Of course, one of the wonderful things about prayer is that we can call out to God at any time. There is actually a limit on the number of 'time-outs' a coach can call during the course of a basketball match. But, praise God, there is no limit to the number of times we can call out to him in prayer.

Jesus said, 'Come to me, all you who are weary and burdened, and I will give you rest' [Matthew 11:28]. Whenever we face problems, difficulties or situations that weigh us down, we can call a 'time-out', knowing that Jesus is waiting to minister to us at the point of our need. And that time of calling out in faith to God can change the whole course of our lives.

Prayer

Thank you, Father, for the privilege of spending time with you.

Help me to make time for you every day.

Lord Jesus, thank you for your open invitation to come to you with my burdens and cares at any time.

As I bring them to you now, I pray that I might know your peace and experience your rest in my life.

Amen.

WHAT'S THE VERDICT?

Throughout its Olympic history, boxing has been plagued by contentious and controversial decisions, which have in turn provoked strong and even violent reactions. For example, at the 1928 Games in Amsterdam, there were extraordinary scenes at the semi-final and final of the bantamweight competition. When Harry Isaacs of South Africa was declared the winner of the semi-final bout, defeating John Daley of the United States, the Americans in the crowd stormed the judges' table. As a result of this 'demonstration never equalled in Olympic history', as the US Official Report described it, the decision was reversed. The reason given was that one of the judges had accidentally transposed his figures for the two fighters. Daley went through to the final, and Isaacs went home in the certain knowledge that he had been robbed.

When it came to the final, Daley failed to produce his best form and was narrowly defeated by Vittorio Tamagnini of Italy. Once again, the Americans in the crowd disgraced themselves. One British reporter described the scene thus: 'For more than two hours, there was little else save din and clatter, screeching and raving, and several skirmishes with the police…' This time, however, the verdict stood.

There have often been accusations of biased judging, in some cases justifiably so. This was particularly the case at the 1960 Games in Rome, where half of the 30 boxing referees and judges were fired! The Koreans, who hosted the 1988 Games in Seoul, believed that several of their boxers had been the victims of biased judging at the 1984 Los Angeles Games. When American flyweight Michael Carbajal was awarded a narrow decision over the Korean boxer Oh Kwang-soo, the favourite for the gold medal, all those feelings of discontent that had been festering away for four years re-surfaced. Matters came to a head the following day, quite literally! Bantamweight Byun Jong-il of Korea was defeated by Alexander Hristov of Bulgaria due to penalty points deducted from Byun's score for illegal use of the head.

Neutrals thought that Hristov was equally guilty, but that didn't excuse what happened next. On this occasion, it wasn't the crowd that attacked the referee – it was the Korean boxing officials! Upon hearing the verdict, Korean boxing coach Lee Hong-soo leapt into the ring and attacked referee Keith Walker of New Zealand, hitting him on the back. Other angry

Koreans followed suit, swinging punches at the hapless Walker, who had to be rescued by his fellow referees as the security guards gradually restored order and cleared the ring. Byun, who still couldn't believe the decision, sat down in the middle of the ring and refused to leave. After 35 minutes, someone brought him a chair! He remained there for 67 minutes, much of it in darkness, before he was finally persuaded to end his protest.

Being a referee, umpire or judge in any sport is often a thankless task. Most officials are not biased, and are trying to be fair to everyone in their application of the laws. Yet, many wrong decisions are made and wrong verdicts announced. And the same is true in life as in sport, which is why Jesus tells us not to judge [Matthew 7:1]; we are to leave that to God, who is the only one in a position to judge people fairly and without bias. And in any case, we are in no position to judge anyone else, being sinners ourselves, a point which Paul makes clear in his letter to the Romans [2:1]. Only God is holy and without sin. Therefore, it is he alone who has the right to judge.

And the holy Judge has indeed applied his laws to us, and has announced his decision: 'This is the verdict: Light has come into the world, but men loved darkness instead of light because their deeds were evil' [John 3:19]. We have broken God's laws by our actions, and have incurred the wrath of the all-seeing, all-knowing, unbiased Judge [Romans 1:18-32]. Yet, amazingly, this Judge loves us and doesn't want us to be condemned; so he has provided for our salvation, no matter who we are or what we have done [John 3:16-18].

And having come to the Light, may we come to love the Light as much as we once loved the darkness, and truly live our lives as 'children of the light' [Ephesians 5:8-11].

Prayer

Lord God, I thank you that although you are my Judge, you are also my loving heavenly Father; that although I deserve your wrath and condemnation, you have provided a way of salvation for me through your Son Jesus.

Please forgive me for the times I have judged others instead of leaving that to you.

Thank you, Lord Jesus, that you shone your light into my life, and drew me to you.

May my love for you grow as I walk in your light all the days of my life.

Amen.

NO MATTER WHAT

The last performer in the final gymnastics competition of the 1968 Games held in Mexico City was Vera Čáslavská of Czechoslovakia. The event was the floor exercises and Čáslavská thrilled the crowd by performing her routine to the tune of The Mexican Hat Dance. She was undoubtedly the female gymnast of the Games, retaining her Olympic title in the All-Around competition and winning a total of four gold and two silver medals, to add to the three gold and two silver she had won at the 1964 Games in Tokyo.

Čáslavská was in fact placed equal first with Larissa Petrik of the Soviet Union in the floor exercises. When she stood alongside Petrik on the podium at the medal ceremony, something very significant happened. The national anthems of both countries were played, starting with Czechoslovakia's. While the Soviet Union's anthem was being played, Čáslavská bowed her head and turned away.

This did not go down too well with the Communist authorities back home; but what she did can hardly have come as a surprise to them. Back in April, she had signed the Manifesto of 2000 Words, which rejected the involvement of the Soviet Union in Czechoslovakia. On 21 August, Soviet tanks had rolled into Prague, the capital city of Czechoslovakia. At the time, Čáslavská was away at a training camp in the district of Moravia. Friends advised her that if she returned to Prague, she would probably be arrested, so she went into hiding in the small town of Šumperk in the Jeseníky mountains. The Olympics were to take place in October, so Čáslavská kept herself fit and in good shape by swinging from the branches of trees, and practised her floor exercise routine in a meadow! In September, the Government decided to allow her to go to Mexico.

Čáslavská may have been a star at the Olympics, but back home she suffered at the hands of the Communist authorities because of her public support for the Manifesto. They made it clear to her that she would never get a job until she publicly repudiated it. This she steadfastly refused to do. On 3 January every year she would go to the office of Antonin Himmel, the Czechoslovak minister for sport, and ask for a coaching job with the national team; and every year she would be turned down.

However, in 1975 he did relent slightly, allowing her to coach at a local club, provided she did not leave the country. But the authorities would still not allow foreign journalists to interview her. By the time communism collapsed in 1989, Čáslavská had defied the authorities for 21 years. When the new regime was established, she was appointed president of the Czech National Olympic Committee.

Vera Čáslavská was fully prepared to stand by her beliefs, no matter what she suffered as a result. All across the world today, literally millions of Christians are suffering far greater persecution at the hands of various governments, dictatorships and authorities because of their faith in Christ. Many of them are experiencing persecution, torture, imprisonment, and even death.

Paul tells us that we are all part of the body of Christ, and reminds us that 'If one part suffers, every part suffers with it' [1 Corinthians 12:26]. The writer to the Hebrews exhorts us to 'Remember those in prison as if you were their fellow-prisoners, and those who are ill-treated as if you yourselves were suffering' [13:3]. How we need to support and pray for our brothers and sisters throughout the world who are persecuted today.

Although most of us will not be put to death for our faith in Christ, we can all expect to face persecution or hostility in some form or another. This is because of our witness to the Gospel, our allegiance to Christ, and our stand for what is right in God's sight in a world whose culture, outlook, values, morals and lifestyle are completely at odds with God's righteousness. But, praise God, we are not alone in times of such opposition. Jesus himself is walking with us and strengthening us, since he knows and understands that we are suffering because of our commitment to him [Matthew 5:11; John 15:18-21]. Vera Čáslavská's reward came on earth; ours awaits us in heaven [Matthew 5:12].

Prayer

Father God, I lift up to you today all my brothers and sisters throughout the world who are suffering because they love you.

Please strengthen, comfort and sustain them, wherever they may be.

Help me also to remain true to you, and to stand up for you, no matter what.

Thank you, Jesus, for walking with me.

Amen.

SETTLING THE SCORE

Mary Lou Retton, the United States gymnast, prepared herself for the most important vault of her life. It would decide whether she or her close rival, Ecaterina Szabó of Romania, won the gold medal in the All-Around competition at the 1984 Games in Los Angeles. Retton needed a score better than 9.95 to win. The partisan crowd was hushed, hoping that their favourite could emulate the perfect ten score that she had achieved in the floor exercise. Watching nervously from the sidelines was Retton's coach, Béla Karolyi.

At one point during the competition, Karolyi jumped over the press barricade to congratulate his protégé on her performance. Ellen Berger of East Germany, head of the technical committee of the International Gymnastics Federation, instructed the US team officials to remind Karolyi that, as he wasn't actually a member of the US coaching squad, he wasn't allowed onto the competition floor. She warned that if Karolyi repeated his offence, she would apply the rules strictly and deduct three-tenths of a point from Retton's score. On hearing this, Karolyi snorted, "She doesn't have the guts to do it here with 10,000 screaming Americans." And so saying, he went off to practise his jump over the barricade!

Retton made her vault and the judges awarded her the perfect ten. She had won the gold medal by 0.05 of a point! Karolyi was right: Berger did not impose the penalty she had threatened when he did leap over the barricade to embrace Retton on her success. To do so would have cost Retton the gold. But Berger did not forget how Karolyi had defied her and would take her revenge four years later.

At the 1988 Games in Seoul, Karolyi was one of the US coaches, while Berger of East Germany was still head of the technical committee of the International Gymnastics Federation. In the Team Combined Exercises, it soon became clear that the Soviet Union was going to take the gold and Romania the silver. East Germany was expected to win the bronze, but the US team was pushing them all the way. It was getting very tense.

Kelly Garrison-Steves of the United States team mounted to perform her routine on the asymmetric bars. Rhonda Faehn of the US removed the springboard used by gymnasts to mount the bars; but instead of then leaving the competition platform completely as the rules stated, she remained at the edge of the platform to watch Garrison-Steves. Berger immediately pointed out that the rules had been infringed and imposed a penalty of five-tenths of a point. In the end, that deduction cost the USA the bronze medal; the East Germans won it by three-tenths of a point! Although technically correct, this ruling had rarely, if ever, been imposed and Berger's decision was generally considered to be rather petty. Not surprisingly, Karolyi was very angry. In his rage he called Berger a 'cow' and the ruling 'a Communist plot'! Berger had certainly got her revenge, with not one but six gymnasts suffering as a result of what she did.

Someone once said, "Don't get mad: get even!" And if we are honest, this is often our first reaction when someone treats us wrongly. We bristle at the thought that somebody might have got one over on us, and we set out to settle the score. How often do we hear people saying words to the effect that they were just paying somebody back for what they had done to them?

But Jesus has some tough things to say to us on this score. For example, 'Do not take revenge on someone who wrongs you' [Matthew 5:39 GNB]. He follows this up by saying that we should not retaliate or seek revenge against anyone, even where to do so would be within our civil rights. And we are certainly not to take the law into our own hands [Matthew 5:38-42]. Paul puts it this way in his letter to the Romans: 'Do not repay anyone evil for evil … Do not take revenge, my friends … Do not be overcome by evil, but overcome evil with good' [Romans 12:17, 19, 21].

Ellen Berger changed the score to settle her score with Béla Karolyi. Jesus expects us to respond in a different way; in a costly way; in a way totally unexpected by those who have wronged us. Our response is to be characterised by gentleness, love and generosity of spirit at all times and in all situations, even when we are unjustly treated. And if my experience is anything to go by, this is one of the greatest challenges we are required to meet.

Prayer

Father God, how I need your strength to help me to respond to this challenge in the way that you require of me!

Please forgive me for the times I have acted wrongly, and sought to take revenge.

May the fruit of your Spirit so grow within me that I treat everyone with gentleness, love and generosity of spirit in all situations.

Amen.

SELFLESS SACRIFICE

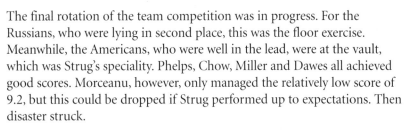

Kerri Strug was about to become a national heroine. She was a somewhat unlikely candidate for such an accolade, being rather more of a support gymnast in the US team than one of their leading lights. She had been a member of the team that won the bronze medal at the 1992 Games in Barcelona, but events in Atlanta four years later were to propel her firmly into the limelight.

The final rotation of the team competition was in progress. For the Russians, who were lying in second place, this was the floor exercise. Meanwhile, the Americans, who were well in the lead, were at the vault, which was Strug's speciality. Phelps, Chow, Miller and Dawes all achieved good scores. Morceanu, however, only managed the relatively low score of 9.2, but this could be dropped if Strug performed up to expectations. Then disaster struck.

Strug attempted a Yurchenko one-and-a-half twist, a vault she had done successfully many times before. However, to everyone's amazement, she didn't get it right and fell awkwardly on landing. The fact that she only scored 9.162 was bad enough, but far worse was what had happened to her left ankle. As she landed, Strug heard something snap, and then experienced excruciating pain shooting up her leg. She hobbled off to the side, knowing that she had less than a couple of minutes in which to decide whether to vault again, or to let Morceanu's score of 9.2 stand.

Strug told her team-mates, "I can't do it. I can't feel my leg." It later transpired that she had sustained a lateral sprain and two torn ligaments in her ankle. Her coach, a certain Béla Karolyi, informed her, "We need a 9.6." Her team-mates, who were not aware how serious Strug's injury actually was, implored her to go for it. And go for it she did.

On completing the vault, she hopped a couple of times on her right foot and then collapsed in agony on the floor. But she had scored 9.712. A soft cast was put on her leg and she was carried to the rostrum by Karolyi to receive her gold medal alongside her jubilant team-mates, to the wild cheers of the partisan home crowd *(see photo on page 56)*.

The television reports in the USA took the line that Strug had sacrificed herself for the team; only because of her second vault had victory been assured. This was true but it was not quite as simple as that. Admittedly, the Russians were still performing, but everyone in the hall knew that the US had already won before Strug made her second vault. She was desperate to qualify for the All-Around final for the first time at the Olympics and to do that she needed a better score in the vault. This she had succeeded in achieving but, to her chagrin, she had to withdraw due to the ankle injury.

Although there might have been a hint of selfishness in Strug's sacrifice for her friends, Jesus' sacrifice for us was pure selflessness. In his gospel, John records Jesus making it quite clear that he sacrificed his life voluntarily for us: 'I am the good shepherd. The good shepherd lays down his life for the sheep…No-one takes it from me, but I lay it down of my own accord' [John 10:11,18]. And Jesus offers this sacrifice as proof of his selfless love for us: 'Greater love has no-one than this, that one lay down his life for his friends' [John 15:13]. Paul talks about how Jesus 'loved us and gave himself up for us as a fragrant offering and sacrifice to God' [Ephesians 5:2]. And this selfless sacrifice on our behalf was offered solely to bring us back to God and to bring us peace with God [1 Peter 3:18; Isaiah 53:5].

But this selfless sacrifice demands another. Jesus said, 'If anyone would come after me, he must deny himself and take up his cross daily and follow me' [Luke 9:23]. The hymn-writer, Isaac Watts, puts it like this: 'Love so amazing, so divine, demands my soul, my life, my all'. In his first letter, John explains how this sacrificial commitment is to be worked out in our lives. He talks about laying down our lives for others, and showing God's love to the needy by providing for them from our own personal resources. He then gently presents us with this challenge: 'Dear children, let us not love with words or tongue, but with actions and in truth' [1 John 3:16-18]. May we respond to this by living our lives as true children of God.

Prayer

Thank you, Jesus, for laying down your life for me.

Father God, I thank you for making it possible through Jesus' selfless sacrifice for me to come back to you, and for the peace that comes with your forgiveness.

I lay my life as a sacrifice before you. Please help me to truly live as your child, whatever sacrifices that may require of me.

Amen.

LITTLE AND LARGE

Dwight Stones of the USA was the overwhelming favourite to win the gold medal in the high jump event at the 1976 Montreal Games. He had won the bronze medal at the 1972 Games in Munich and he was now the world record holder. But he had one little foible that was to have a large effect on his performance: the fear of rain. This was because his technique involved approaching the bar at high speed – far quicker than any of his fellow competitors. He needed it to be dry underfoot, and this became an obsession with him. Imagine his frustration and anger then, when he found out that the stadium in Montreal had not been completed as originally conceived. Plans for a retractable roof, which would have kept out any rain, had been shelved. And, sure enough, as the high jump competition moved towards its climax, it began to rain.

Soon, there were puddles all over the apron of the high jump area. Unimpressed by the efforts of the officials to get rid of the water, Stones grabbed hold of a squeegee himself and began to mop the area frantically. Although others joined in with him, it was a hopeless task. Stones was beaten before he made another jump. He finished up with the bronze medal, his best jump being all of four inches below his world record. The surprise winner, Jacek Wszola of Poland, was asked when he realised he would win. His reply was, "When it started to rain." In Philadelphia four days later, Stones set a new world record for the high jump.

It wasn't the prospect of rain that bothered Mike Gebhardt and his fellow competitors in the sailboard competition; it was the problem of rubbish floating in the harbour. Before the 1992 Games began in Barcelona, many complaints were made about the state of the Parc de Mar venue where the sailing events were to be held. The whole area was polluted by all manner of garbage and waste, including refrigerators and dead rats!

The organisers eventually acquiesced to the demands of the International Yacht Racing Union and dispatched four vessels to collect the rubbish in the harbour each day. But some of it was missed, as Gebhardt was about to find out.

As the seventh race of the sailboarding event began, the American looked favourite to take the gold medal. But then, disaster struck on the final lap; a plastic bin bag got caught on his sailboard. As Gebhardt frantically tried to get rid of it, he was passed by six other competitors, which meant that he finished up in the silver medal position. His dreams of gold had been thwarted, not by the skill of his opponents – but by a bin bag! Such a little thing; such a large effect.

Many of the problems that we experience start off as little things. But if we don't deal with them properly at that stage, they can soon assume large proportions and have a damaging effect on our lives. In my experience, fear and habits fall into this category. Jesus warned us to be on our guard against such little things as an angry thought and a lustful look because, unless they are dealt with, murder and adultery can be the result. He also spoke dramatically about the need for us to be ruthless with any and every little thing in our lives that might cause us to sin [Matthew 5:21-30]. As Paul reminds us, all the devil needs to hinder our spiritual progress is something as little as a foothold [Ephesians 4:27].

Sad to say, it is often little things that can cause trouble in our churches. Paul had to write to the church in Rome about a particular issue that was dividing the people into two distinct camps: food. They were always at loggerheads over which foods it was permissible to eat, and which it wasn't. We can imagine Paul groaning with frustration as he wrote pleadingly, 'Do not destroy the work of God for the sake of food' [Romans 14:20].

I wonder how often in our churches we are guilty of something similar? Of course serious issues, concerning for example false doctrine and immorality, must be confronted: but how often does the family of God polarise into opposite camps over little disagreements that don't really matter? How many churches have split apart over relatively minor issues, to the detriment of the Gospel witness in the community? It seems to me that Paul's entreaty to the people of God is as relevant today as it was then.

Prayer

Father God, thank you for reminding me to be on the look-out for little things in my life that need to be dealt with.

Please help me to be ruthless with every little thing that could cause me to sin, so that I don't give the devil a foothold.

I pray for my church, that we will be a united force for you in our community, and not be torn apart by little issues that don't really matter.

Amen.

A CUNNING PLAN

Jim Ryun of the United States went to the 1968 Olympics as the clear favourite to win the gold medal in the 1500 metres. He held the world record for that distance and had not been beaten for three years. However, the Games were being held at Mexico City. This high altitude venue, with its thinner air, would prove helpful to the sprinters, but have adverse effects on those athletes running the longer distances who were not used to such conditions. Such considerations meant that Kip Keino of Kenya was likely to pose a threat to Ryun.

All the athletes knew that Ryun's greatest asset was his devastating finishing kick. Keino's plan was to get so far ahead of him during the first three laps that Ryun wouldn't be able to catch him. With the help of his fellow Kenyan, Ben Jipcho, who sacrificed himself as Keino's pacemaker, the plan was carried out. Keino passed the 800 metre mark in the unbelievable time of 1 minute 55.3 seconds, well ahead of the pack. The stunned crowd waited for Keino to blow up, but amazingly he kept going. He won by a massive 20 metres in an Olympic record time of 3 minutes 34.9 seconds, a staggering time considering the race was run at altitude, with Ryun in second place. The plan had been a complete success.

Twenty years later, in the swimming pool, the final of the 200 metres freestyle at the Seoul Games was expected to be a straight contest between Michael Gross of Germany, the defending Olympic champion and world record holder, and Matt Biondi of the United States, the world record holder in the 100 metres freestyle. But Lawrie Laurence, who coached outsider Duncan Armstrong of Australia, had other ideas.

Armstrong was to swim in lane 6, next to Biondi in lane 5. Laurence devised a plan accordingly. Assuming that Biondi would go off quickly as usual, Armstrong was to save his energy by swimming as close to Biondi's lane as he could. This would allow him to slipstream in the wake of the 6-feet 6-inch American. The plan worked brilliantly. As Armstrong said later, "I just sucked into his trough and bodysurfed the first 100 metres." On the final leg, Armstrong passed Anders Holmertz of Sweden, who finished second, and then Biondi himself, who finished third, to win in a new world record time. Gross finished fifth.

The bantamweight freestyle wrestling final at the 1996 Atlanta Games saw a contest between Kendall Cross of the USA and Giuvi Sissaouri of Canada. Before the Games began, Cross's coach, Zeke Jones, was sure that Sissaouri would reach the final, so he planned accordingly. Knowing him to be a dangerous opponent, Jones studied tapes of Sissaouri's fights and adopted his style in coaching sessions, so Cross would be fully prepared and know what to expect. The plan worked superbly. Cross countered every move made by his opponent and was able to defeat him, thus winning the gold.

Paul warns us that we too have a dangerous opponent, who is intent on planning our downfall. He urges us to 'Put on the full armour of God so that you can take your stand against the devil's schemes' [Ephesians 6:11]. But, as Paul says in another letter, 'we are not unaware of his schemes' [2 Corinthians 2:11]. Like Kendall Cross, we can be well prepared for the tactics our opponent will use.

The devil's cunning plan, as revealed in Genesis 3, contains various elements. He questions the truth of God's Word, lies and twists what God has said, putting doubt into our minds. He plays on our weaknesses to get us to do things God has forbidden. He sows seeds of suspicion and mistrust to break up our relationship with God. He tempts us into doing and thinking things we shouldn't. Everything he says sounds very plausible and, before we know it, we've pressed the self-destruct rather than the eject button! He even tries to get at others through us and seeks to stir up strife in an effort to break up the family of God.

Thus forewarned, clad in the 'armour of God' and empowered by the Spirit, we can successfully counter all of 'the devil's schemes' and see him defeated. However, there is a danger that we could allow ourselves to become complacent, so it is as well for us to bear in mind Paul's concern for the Corinthians: 'But I am afraid that just as Eve was deceived by the serpent's cunning, your minds may somehow be led astray from your sincere and pure devotion to Christ' [2 Corinthians 11:3].

Prayer

Father God, thank you for providing me with the armour, the power, and all the information I need to be able to counter the devil's cunning and defeat him.

Please help me to be constantly on my guard against his schemes, that I may not fall prey to his plan and be led astray.

Amen.

LIFE-CHANGING

On 9 July 1922, Johnny Weissmuller of the USA made history by becoming the first person to swim 100 metres in under a minute. In February 1924, he set a record time of 57.4 seconds, a time which remained unbeaten for the next ten years. At the Paris Games that same year, he won a gold in the 100 and 400 metres freestyle events, as well as in the 4 x 200 metres relay. Four years later in Amsterdam, he repeated the achievement in the 100 metres and the 200 metres relay, making a total of five Olympic gold medals.

Weissmuller intended to swim at the 1932 Games in Los Angeles as well, but in 1930 he was offered $500 a week to work for the BVD Underwear Company advertising swimsuits. One of his BVD photos was noticed in Hollywood, and that was to change his life. He was invited for a screen test, after which he was soon offered the part of Tarzan. Instead of performing in the pool in 1932, he was performing on the cinema screen in his first film, *Tarzan, the Ape Man*. He played the role in 11 more films over the next 16 years *(see photo on page 56)*.

In the eyes of the world, Weissmuller was Tarzan. In 1959, he was in Cuba for a celebrity golf tournament. On the way to the course, the car in which he was travelling with friends and bodyguards was held up by a band of Fidel Castro's guerrillas. All the occupants were bundled out and rifles trained on them. It was a very tense moment; they all thought they were about to die. Weissmuller decided to do what he did best: he raised himself slowly to his full height and beat his chest with his fists, emitting his famous Tarzan yell! The guerrillas stared in disbelief, then cried out in sheer delight, "Tarzan! Tarzan! Welcome to Cuba!" They dropped their rifles and gathered round him, shaking him by the hand and asking excitedly for his autograph. They then escorted his car to the golf course.

Jealous of MGM's instant success with Weissmuller as Tarzan, Paramount Studios decided to recruit an Olympic star. They sent agents to the 1932 Games in Los Angeles, and eventually decided on the swimmer Buster Crabbe. The American had won the gold in the 400 metres freestyle by a mere one-tenth of a second from the favourite, Jean Taris of France. As Crabbe said later, "That one-tenth of a second changed my life." It was then the Hollywood producers "discovered latent histrionic abilities in me". He starred first as Tarzan, and then Buck Rogers and Flash Gordon.

Gideon's encounter with the angel of the Lord lasted rather longer than one-tenth of a second, but it also changed his life, thrusting him into a starring role as leader of the Israelites in their battle against the Midianites [Judges 6-7]. He was furtively threshing wheat in a winepress when the angel appeared to him. The angel addressed him with the unlikely words, 'mighty warrior' [6:12]. Gideon probably looked round to see who the angel was talking to! He took some convincing that it was he who was the mighty warrior in God's sight. I'm sure he didn't feel like a mighty warrior; far from it. In fact, he probably felt afraid, isolated, weak, unable to cope, in despair, lacking in faith, and totally overwhelmed by the situation in which he found himself. He probably saw himself as a complete failure; but that's not how God saw him.

As far as the cinema-going public was concerned, Weissmuller and Crabbe were actually Tarzan, Buck Rogers and Flash Gordon. As far as God is concerned, each one of us is actually a mighty warrior, although we may often feel like Gideon did. But, like Gideon, we need to realise that being a mighty warrior is not something we can achieve in our own strength; we are mighty warriors because God is with us [Judges 6:12,16].

It is nothing to do with how we may feel or how we may see ourselves. It is all to do with the fact that God is with us, enabling us, in and through his strength, to be mighty warriors in whatever situation we find ourselves; and, like Gideon, to emerge triumphant.

Prayer

Father God, thank you for the encouragement that there is in the story of Gideon.

Please help me always to see myself as you see me, and to realise that I am a mighty warrior because you are with me.

May I face the situations which cause me to fear or despair with renewed confidence, knowing that in and through your strength I will emerge triumphant.

Amen.

Paul certainly understood this, and proved it to be true in the many trials he faced. He affirmed his confidence in God with these faith-inspiring words: 'I can do everything through him who gives me strength…' [Philippians 4:13]. 'If God is for us, who can be against us?' [Romans 8:31]. Let's see ourselves as God sees us. It's a life-changing experience.

GOLDEN GOAL

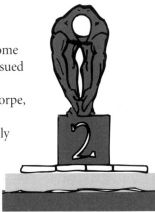

At the 2000 Games in Sydney, there were some problems with the passes that had been issued to allow access to the Olympic village. Australian swimmers, Grant Hackett and Ian Thorpe, were among those athletes who were inconvenienced by this fiasco. Hackett was initially denied entry on the grounds that other 'Grant Hacketts' had already been allowed in! They had apparently shown security staff fake passes with Hackett's name and photo on them.

Thorpe was one of several members of the Australian team, including 400 metres runner Cathy Freeman, to find out that they had been given false identity passes. Returning to the village, triumphant after winning several gold medals in the pool, Thorpe had problems with the bar code on his pass. It was only when he showed the security staff his gold medals that they let him in!

Praise God we won't need to show an identity pass to get into heaven! He knows each one of us by name [John 10:3]. Unlike boxer Pascual Pérez of Argentina, we will not be confused with someone else. At the 1948 London Games, Pérez was disqualified from the flyweight competition for being overweight before he had even entered the ring. Later, it transpired that the officials had confused him with Arnoldo Pares, a bantamweight from the same country. Pérez was re-instated and went on to win the gold medal!

Nor, according to the Bible, will we be admitted to heaven on the grounds of what we can show we have achieved, or because of the good deeds we have done – as commendable as all that might be. Unlike a gold medal, heaven is not a goal which can be achieved through our own efforts. Access comes only through the grace of God, who has provided Jesus to be our Saviour [Ephesians 2:8-9]. All we have to do is to repent and receive his forgiveness. Entry into heaven is a matter of what we have *received*, not what we have *achieved*.

Hackett, Thorpe and Pérez all achieved their golden goal. So did American swimmer, Michael Barrowman. When he got back to his home after winning gold in the 200 metres freestyle at the 1992 Games, he found a rather unusual surprise awaiting him. In celebration of his achievement, his neighbours had painted the whole of his front lawn gold!

Never mind a lawn of gold; the Bible gives us a picture of heaven which includes a street of gold in a city of gold! [Revelation 21:18,21]. A golden goal indeed! And what a wonderful celebration there will be when Jesus, the champion of heaven, calls us home to be with him for ever! Our Olympics of Life complete, we can look forward to those words, which will mean more than any gold medal: 'Well done, good and faithful servant!'

Prayer

Thank you, Father God, for your wonderful plan of salvation.

Thank you, Lord Jesus, that through your death you have made it possible for each one of us to be accepted into heaven.

I look forward to the day when I shall be in your glorious presence for ever.

Amen.

THEMES INDEX

INDEX OF BIBLE REFERENCES

Abbreviations: GNB - Good News Bible, AV - Authorised Version.